The
Bench
and the Bar

The Bench and the Bar

A Centennial View Of Denver's Legal History

By Alan J. Kania and Diane Hartman

Pictorial Research by Dwight Swanson

*"The Judiciary" and "Spotlight on Legal Sponsors"
by Janet Layne*

*Produced in cooperation with
the Denver Bar Association*

Windsor Publications, Inc.—History Book Division
Managing Editor: Karen Story
Design Director: Ellen Ifrah
Photo Director: Susan L. Wells
Executive Editor: Pamela Schroeder

Staff for *The Bench and the Bar*
Senior Manuscript Editor: Jerry Mosher
Photo Editor: Robin Sterling
Copy Editor: Teri Davis Greenberg
Senior Editor, Corporate Biographies: Jeffrey Reeves
Production Editor, Corporate Biographies: Lisa Woo
Proofreader: Annette Nibblett Arrieta
Customer Service Manager: Phyllis Feldman-Schroeder
Editorial Assistants: Elizabeth Anderson, Alex Arredondo, Kate Coombs, Lori Erbaugh, Darlene
    Huckabey, Wilma Huckabey
Publisher's Representatives, Corporate Biographies: John Compton, Joyce Everhart
Layout Artist, Corporate Biographies: Bonnie Felt
Layout Artist, Editorial: Michael Burg

Library of Congress Cataloging-in-Publication Data
Kania, Alan J.
The bench and the bar : a centennial view of Denver's legal history / by Alan J. Kania and
    Diane Hartman; pictorial research by Dwight Swanson ; "The judiciary" and "Spotlight on
    legal sponsors" by Janet Layne. — 1st ed.
p. 184 cm. 22 x 28
  "Produced in cooperation with the Denver Bar Association."
Includes bibliographical references and index.
ISBN 0-89781-439-8

1. Denver Bar Association—History. 2. Justice, Administration of—Colorado—Denver—History.
    3. Denver (Colo.)—History—Sources. I. Layne, Janet. II. Title.
KF334.D46D4646 1991   91-4149
340'.06'078883–dc20   CIP

Contents

An era of adventure and discovery, the 1860s
saw the need for an organized legal community
and soon the seeds of the Denver Bar Association began to grow. Courtesy, Colorado Historical Society

PRESIDENTS' MESSAGE

We are pleased to present *The Bench and the Bar* as part of the Denver Bar Association's centennial celebration.

Walk with us through more than 100 years of history about Denver's legal community. Meet some of the larger-than-life characters who practiced law when Denver was a dusty tent town at the confluence of Cherry Creek and the Platte River.

We believe you'll find this history entertaining. But most importantly, we think readers will understand why we feel a sense of pride about what Denver attorneys have accomplished during our first century of service to the legal profession and to the community.

With admiration for our founders and with pride in our heritage, we look forward to the next 100 years.

Jane Michaels
President, 1990-1991
Denver Bar Association

Ben Aisenberg
President, 1991-1992
Denver Bar Association

ACKNOWLEDGMENTS

The authors wish to thank the following people for reading the manuscript, offering suggestions, or submitting to interviews: Tom Noel, Larry Weiss, Walter A. Steele, Charles C. Turner, Jonathan D. Asher, Judge John L. Kane, Jr., Justice Edward E. Pringle, Robert B. Yegge, Chief Justice Luis D. Rovira, Peter F. Breitenstein, Philip G. Dufford, Robert H. Harry, J.W. Tracey, Forrest B. O'Dell, Arthur C. Underwood, Dean Dennis O. Lynch, Thompson Marsh, Charles S. Vigil, Anthony Zarlengo, Kathi Rudolph, David Brand, and Gina Weitzenkorn.

Thanks also to the Denver Public Library Western History Collection, the Colorado State Historical Society, the State Judicial Library, the archive librarians of the Denver Post, photo archivist Dwight Swanson, and photographer Steve Zavodny.

Special thanks go to the Denver Bar Association History Book Committee: William C. McClearn, chair, and members Garth C. Grissom and Royal C. Rubright and the Centennial Committee, chaired by Dale R. Harris, and Jane Michaels, president of the DBA 1990-1991.

Our heartfelt thanks to Howard Tallman and his firm, Holland & Hart, for their legal help. When our original publishers declared bankruptcy and publication of this book (scheduled for 1991) seemed elusive, Howard took the lead in solving the problems so the book could become reality.

Chronology:
100 Years of the Denver Bar Association

This chronology, although certainly incomplete, should give an idea of some of the highlights in the first 100 years of the Denver Bar Association.

1891

On Halloween, 125 men assemble at the Odd Fellows Hall, 1545 Champa Street, for the first meeting of the Denver Bar Association.

1892

The first class of the law school of the University of Denver is held. A small group of law students attends. Upon graduation, all pass their bar examinations and are admitted to practice.

1898

U.S. District Judge Moses Hallett does not admit Mary Lathrop to federal practice in the U.S. District Court because he doesn't believe women should practice law.

1901

American Bar Association annual convention is held in Denver.

1903

The Denver Bar Association adopts a code of ethics (already adopted by the Colorado Bar Association). Listed are 55 general rules, with the note that there are "pitfalls and man-traps at every step."

After the panic of 1893, Denver businessmen sought to diversify the local economy so that the city could become a true regional center. Although much of the city's mineral wealth disappeared, it was gradually replaced by manufacturing and other industries. This Denver street scene was photographed around the turn of the century. Courtesy, Colorado Historical Society

1903

The Denver Bar Association passes resolutions against professional jury service.

1907

The nation's first juvenile court is founded in Denver by Judge Ben Lindsey.

1907

The Denver Bar Association establishes a law library.

1912

Westminster Law School begins in the old Academy of Medicine building, offering night classes. The first graduating class will be in 1915.

1914

On April 10, the Denver Law Club is founded.

1923

For the first time the medical and legal professions hold a joint meeting. Three hundred doctors and lawyers dine together and discuss mutual concerns.

1923

The Denver Bar Association *Record*, renamed *Dicta* in 1928, appears as a four-page bulletin. It later "developed into a modest pamphlet of unpretentious appearance." This monthly bulletin gave a notice of the next meeting, reports of Denver Bar Association committees, financial reports, and any other news the bar thought members might need.

1923

Members of the Denver Bar Association work for an amendment to the Colorado constitution that would remove a $5,000 limitation on the annual compensation of the justices of the Colorado Supreme Court and a $4,000 limitation for district judges.

1924

A Denver Bar Association committee begins studying conditions of the jails in Denver. "Incarceration in them cannot fail to injure both the health and character of the prisoners," it says.

1925

The Legal Aid Society is founded to represent people too poor to hire lawyers. This fills a void left when the legal aid dispensary, begun 20 years earlier by the University of Denver College of Law, suspended operations because of increasing costs.

1926

The American Bar Association National Convention is held in Denver. Delegates vote to approve an act to regulate the sale and possession of firearms to curb the rise in crime. Eighteen women lawyers attend the conference; the three from Denver include Mary Lathrop, Mabelle Carter, and Bertha Perry. ABA President Chester

William B. Miller served as the first full-time secretary of the Denver and Colorado Bar Associations. Courtesy, Colorado Bar Association

Gambling, one of the favorite pastimes of the Wild West, was no longer legal in twentieth-century Colorado. In 1935 Police Chief George W. Marland (far left) and Manager of Safety William E. Guthner (center) personally helped destroy a pile of confiscated slot machines. Courtesy, Colorado Historical Society

Long welcomes more than 2,000 to the convention, setting a record. (Membership in the ABA was about 25,000.)

1928

At a meeting of the medical society and the Denver Bar Association, W.M. Bond tells five stories of "increasing intensity, much to the amusement of the men present and somewhat to the embarrassment of the four ladies present." Attendance included 143 doctors and 144 lawyers. At the annual banquet, some wag reported that "the judges were more interesting than was expected."

1928

The annual Denver Bar Association dinner is discontinued and the "annual picnic" begins. A "Bar-B-Q" is held at Mt. Vernon Country Club.

1929

The U.S. Circuit Court of Appeals for the Tenth Circuit is organized.

1930

Denver Bar Association members decide to hold a bar primary in which they will select candidates for the district bench. Great secrecy surrounds the process. The bar actively promotes their choices, distributing 70,000 booklets to "practically every home in the city." The bar raises $3,850 and spends all but $2.73 promoting its selection of judges.

1932

Members vote to pay $75 per month to Lucille Becker for her services as bookkeeper and executive secretary and by way of compensation to Fairfield, Gould and Woods for the space occupied in their office by the bar association records and their expense in providing a telephone for the association's use. (Albert J. Gould is bar president.)

1932

The Denver Bar Association transfers its library, to be housed in the new courthouse, as a gift to the city.

1938

The American Bar Association delegate brings back word that for the first time in the history of that association, the predominant speakers were of the "so-called New

Deal. There was generally a more democratic feeling among lawyers and recognition of the need of a strong left wing in the American Association."

1939

Anna Rankin Waterman, widow of U.S. Senator Charles W. Waterman, dies and leaves to the Denver Bar Association a trust fund, the income from which is to be used to "relieve financial necessities, assuaging the hardships and

time secretary of the Denver and Colorado Bar Associations, with offices in the Odd Fellows Hall. The bar moves to the Chamber of Commerce Building in 1949. That year the Denver Bar Association decides not to object to boldface type used to call attention to attorneys in the phone book.

1951

Terry O'Neill is secretary of the Denver and Colorado Bar Associations until 1954.

When Prohibition passed in Colorado, law enforcement officials were faced with a new problem. Due to the resourcefulness of its producers, liquor was still readily available throughout the state as evidenced by this still, which was confiscated near Greeley. When the still was seized in the early 1930s, it was considered to be one of the largest producers of bootleg liquor in Colorado. Courtesy, Denver Public Library, Western History Department

lightening the financial burdens of aged, infirm or otherwise incapacitated members of the Colorado bar in good repute and standing, practicing for 10 years."

1948

The Denver Bar Association issues the first minimum fee schedule (later discontinued because of serious concerns as to its legality).

1948-1951

William B. Miller is the first full-

1953

Denver judges begin wearing black robes for the first time.

1954

The Denver and Colorado Bar Associations move to the Midland Federal Savings Building at 17th and Glenarm streets and within the year negotiate a lease at 1700 Broadway in the new Mile High Center. The agreement stipulates that the DBA will manage the law library for the building.

An unidentified prisoner peers out from behind the bars of the Denver City Jail. Until the new police building opened in 1940, the city jail was located in the basement of Old City Hall at 14th and Arapahoe. Courtesy, Denver Public Library, Western History Department

1954

A survey by the American Bar Association and Carnegie Foundation about the legal profession finds that lawyers are "good joiners, good social mixers and among the most active and responsible members of the community." Their average income, which is "considerably less than doctors," is $7,532. However, the survey says, lawyers now number more than 200,000 and "lawyers may be the most unpopular persons in the U.S."

1954

Don Molen becomes secretary (later called executive director) of the Denver and Colorado Bar Associations until Bill Miller returns in 1961.

1955

John E. Gorsuch recommends that the Colorado ban on interracial marriages be repealed because it "leads to confusion, misery and often open flouting of the written law."

1956

After much controversy in the legal community, the Colorado Supreme Court decides that judges in lower courts can permit newspaper photography and regulate TV broadcasting of courtroom procedures.

1957

Colorado Supreme Court Chief Justice O. Otto Moore asks for a full judiciary study because of the court backlog.

1957

The Denver Bar Association asks the legislature to remove state judges from politics.

1957

James C. Flanigan, 42, a deputy district attorney, is appointed the eighth municipal judge in Denver by Mayor Will Nicholson. Flanigan is Colorado's first black judge.

1957

There are 28 father/son lawyer teams in Denver, according to

Dicta, the Denver Bar Association publication.

1957

University of Denver College of Law and Westminster Law School merge. All graduates of Westminster receive diplomas from the University of Denver College of Law.

1958

Discipline of lawyers is taken away from the bar association. It will be handled by a committee appointed by the Colorado Supreme Court.

1958

A new Colorado corporation code is proposed.

1958

Legislation is presented by the bar associations that would hospitalize alcoholics rather than jail them.

1958

The American Bar Association president warns the Colorado Bar Association convention of an impending lawyer shortage.

1965

Norma Comstock is elected first woman president of the Denver Bar Association.

1966

The Thursday Night Bar is founded.

1966

A constitutional amendment passes (promoted by the Denver and Colorado Bar Associations, among others) to take judges out of the election process. Judges will now be appointed under a modified "Missouri Plan," sometimes called "merit selection."

1977

The U.S. Supreme Court rules that, under the First Amendment, lawyers have the right to advertise (over the objections of the American Bar Association).

1980

William Miller retires; Charles Turner, director of Continuing Legal Education, is appointed new executive director.

1981

Denver experiences an "oil bust," which sends its economy into a tailspin.

1988

Charles Casteel is elected first black president of the Denver Bar Association.

1988

The first Barristers' Ball raises more than $40,000 for the Thursday Night Bar.

1990

Teen Court program begins.

1991

The Denver Bar Association celebrates 100 years of service.

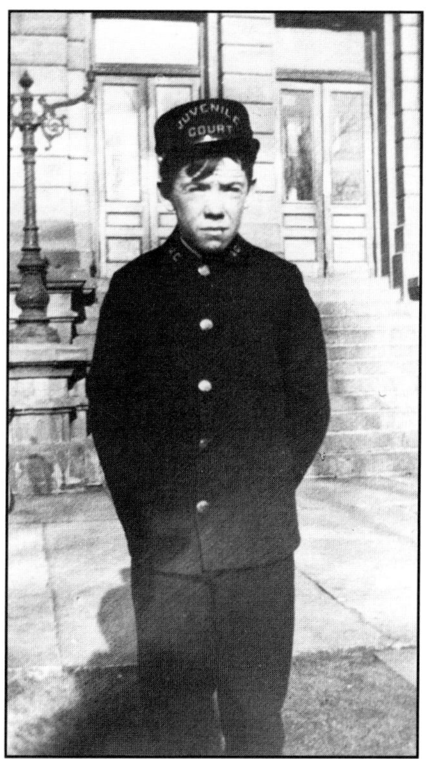

Although Mary Lathrop was concerned with conditions in the state's reformatories and was opposed to Benjamin B. Lindsey's methods of juvenile reform, Denver's Juvenile Court system became a model for others across the nation under the direction of the respected Judge Lindsey. Courtesy, Colorado Historical Society

DENVER'S LEGAL HISTORY

The first rudimentary street in the settlement of Denver City was a cluster of log houses known as "Indian Row." The settlers of 1858 had to haul logs 35 miles across the treeless plains in order to build their spartan cabins. It was around this primitive townsite that the city of Denver began to grow. Courtesy, Denver Public Library, Western History Department

GOLD SEEKING AND LAW MAKING

Prospectors called it "color." That color was shining gold, enticing, alluring, heavy with the promise of an easy life and secure future.

News of a find in the central Rockies spread quickly across an economically depressed country and the rag-tag hordes began to tumble into Colorado.

Thus began the Gold Rush of 1858-1859 and the first round in the boom-bust cycle that Denver has come to know.

One of the first lawyers in the territory, Judge George Hicks, Sr., came only for the gold. Disappointed in what he found, he became one of the "go-backers." Years later, journalist Jerome Smiley remarked that Hicks couldn't be considered one of the pioneer members of the Denver Bar, "though gold seeking was not altogether outside the professional purposes of those who constituted it in pioneer times, nor is it foreign to the inclinations of those who now contribute to its honor and dignity." Some came to find gold; others came to make their fortune from the gold seekers. The land was bleak, wild, and dusty, except in the winter when it was bleak, wild, and frozen. Standing guard over all were the intimidating, inspiring, soaring peaks of the Rocky Mountains. As miners gathered in huge numbers, towns with canvas-roofed buildings bloomed in the shadows of these mountains. Card sharks and lovers of whiskey drew near.

Law was the law of self-preservation.

In 1855, today's Colorado, then variously known as Pike's Peak Country, Arapahoe County, or Kansas Territory, was considered Indian territory. It was too far away from the other territories to be governed by them, although the Rocky Mountain region was, at various times, part of Utah, New Mexico, Kansas, and Nebraska territories.

In 1859 came another rumor, a new gold rush, and more hordes.

To accommodate the swelling population, two towns—Denver City and Auraria—grew up on opposite banks of Cherry Creek, near its confluence with the South Platte River. Settlers decided that the rivalry would encourage healthy competition.

Despite the lure of the Rocky Mountain gold rush, Denver's population hovered around 5,000 during the 1860s. After the arrival of the area's first railroad in 1870, the city's population jumped, and by 1880 it had swelled to about 35,000 residents. Newly arriving settlers are depicted in this 1866 Harper's Magazine *engraving by James F. Gookins. Courtesy, Colorado Historical Society*

Attorney David C. Collier had arrived at the new settlements in 1858 and was the only lawyer for almost a year. This was a time of informal government (technically this area was governed by Kansas Territory) and there was no U.S. court system. Conditions weren't ideal for luring young lawyers west to practice law.

Still, the lawyers—along with a lot of other people—came. One paper said "the woods were full of them." By 1860, the towns had about 30 eating and drinking places, more than 24 stores, and about two dozen doctors and lawyers. Their number included Judge George W. Purkins, J. Bright Smith, Hamilton R. Hunt, Alfred Sayre, H.P.A. Smith, Harley R. Morse, Amos Steck, Moses Hallett, John C. Moore, H.F. Seanett, and James Cavanaugh. They made a scant living as lawyers and often resorted to moonlighting among the miners.

Because of the lack of legal standing, both Denver City and Auraria drew an unsavory transient element, causing both towns to develop notorious reputations. The *Leavenworth Times* reported that "Fights, rows, brawls, shooting and stabbing affrays are the order of the day" in the Cherry Creek towns and "not an evening or a night has passed of late without the shedding of some blood."

Great confusion reigned about the jurisdiction of Denver and Auraria; the towns aspired to create a separate territory rather than accept the weak, distant government of Kansas Territory. Until the confusion cleared, the residents had to rely on their own system of protecting the frontier community from the onslaught of ruffians that began at the end of the 1850s.

A writer in a Denver Bar journal in 1923 commented on pioneer law: "Swifte justice was meted out to the horse thief, to the hold-up and the cheat. More often than not, those assembled to hear the trial acted

as court, judge and jury."

The settlers decided to symbolically circle the wagons. Auraria would join Denver. On a bridge across Cherry Creek, in the middle of the night (April 6, 1859), they joined forces under the name Denver City.

In their effort at self-government, civil matters were pretty much taken care of by "Miners' Courts" and criminal matters were handled by the "People's Courts." During 1859 and 1860, 14 trials for murder were held. Strict procedures were followed, with a jury of 12 men and one to three judges. Only six of the men tried were sentenced to death.

In September 1860, William N. Byers, the editor of the *Rocky Mountain News*, editorialized about the "Necessity of Law":

Recent events in and around this city have shown the great necessity that exists for some kind of government and law. Crime has long stalked throughout the land, but never until within the last two months has all its hideousness been presented to the eye of day.

The situation, Byers said, was truly appalling to "those who value life and property, and more particularly to the many estimable families that have made their homes in our midst."

The *Rocky Mountain News* suggested the formation of a police force, warning that "Delays are dangerous."

Meetings were called ". . . to put a stop to crimes of darkness and dishonesty, which are nowadays being perpetrated in our midst, and in the hopes of effecting a substitute for the 'hanging after night' arrangements."

Few people attended. The local paper fussed and fumed: "The business of Denver is suffering seriously for this crimi-

The lure of gold attracted up to 5,000 immigrants per week to the Denver area in the 1850s and 1860s. Most were just passing through, many chose to stay, and still more were forced to return to their homes after their dreams of wealth eluded them. Courtesy, Colorado Historical Society

After the first reports of Rocky Mountain gold reached the East, many immigrants expected Cherry Creek to be flowing with minerals. The real wealth, they soon found out, was to be found in the mountain mining regions in areas such as Central City and Cripple Creek. Courtesy, Denver Public Library, Western History Department

Appointed as governor of the Territory of Kansas by President Buchanan in 1858, James William Denver (1817-1892) helped to bring order to the mining regions of Colorado, which were then located in the Kansas Territory. It is thought that settler William Larimer suggested the name of Denver for the new townsite in hopes of gaining the governor's support in the local rivalry between the Cherry Creek settlements. Denver is pictured here in 1874. Courtesy, Denver Public Library, Western History Department

nal neglect, and unless a resolute stand is soon taken, our mountain friends will give us a wide berth when their necessities compel them to look for their winter supplies."

Certainly, Denver's leading lawyers were discouraged about the crippled sense of justice in the new town. And probably no court case discouraged them as much as the jurisdictional problems that plagued the trial of James A. Gordon in 1860.

Gordon had apparently staggered into a bar saying "I have killed a damned Dutchman . . . and would kill a thousand more." When he fled town, the sheriff went after him. The problem of jurisdiction got more and more tangled as semi-official local governments got into the act. Was Denver in Arapahoe or Montana County? Could Kansas try him? It wasn't clear. Finally, a trial was held in Denver with much hoopla and emotion. Gordon was pronounced guilty and was hanged.

Denver continued to confront a rash of murders in what the *Rocky Mountain News* called "the crimson epidemic."

A typical case occurred at the end of November 1860, when Thomas Freeman's body, covered with gunshot wounds and bruises, was found floating in a stream. The People's Court gathered witnesses, who gave testimony during a two-day trial, and the court convicted Patrick Waters. A little before 3 p.m. on the third day, the sheriff, deputy sheriff, and a posse escorted Waters to the gallows. He spent a few moments in prayer, confessed his guilt, and was "launched into eternity—the fall broke his neck and instantly ended his sufferings."

Frontier No More

Attempts at government came in fits and starts. For instance, the provisional Jefferson Territory lasted little more than a year.

Finally, Congress acted to give the area a legal government. This was just before the Civil War; when a territory became a state the first question asked was whether the state would stick with the Union. When Texas seceded in 1861 with the rest of the Deep South, Republicans in Congress quickly established territorial governments—with no reference to slavery—for Dakota, Nevada, and Colorado.

In 1861 Colorado's territorial legislature laid out 17 counties, gave Denver a charter, organized courts, and adopted a legal code. It also validated the actions of the improvised local governments.

Denver started shedding its wild ways and became more cosmopolitan as the central business district began to emerge, fringed by residential areas with lawns and trees and Victorian-style architecture.

With a decline in production from the mines, the population of Denver dropped to around 3,000 after the Civil War. Because it was far from other towns, Denver became more isolated. Indians, reacting to the threat to their lands and way of life, began attacking those traveling across the prairies.

In 1871 Colorado was still five years away from being a state. Denver was officially under the jurisdiction of the federal court system because it was still territorial in status. Anyone could call himself a lawyer and the courtroom was a shambles.

Attempts at Beginning a Bar Association

Was it to be dueling judges?

In May 1871, Justice of the Peace Henry A. Clough received a letter containing a challenge from District Judge N. Harrison. Harrison said Clough had accused him of lying and had hurt him personally and professionally. He asked him to retract the statement. Clough read the letter and sent the messenger away with no response.

A second, angrier, letter also drew no response. In it, Harrison asked, "inform me, if I demand of you that satisfaction to which I think I

Colorado's first practicing lawyer was David C. Collier, shown here with his wife in the 1890s. Collier arrived in Denver City in December 1858 and soon became associated with the Denver Town Company. He later served as a clerk of the probate court, and as the superintendent of the state's first Sunday school. Courtesy, Colorado Historical Society

LEFT: In his 1859 journey west, renowned newspaperman Horace Greeley found Denver to be filled with raucous saloons such as the Arcadia, home of Denver's first billiards table. Greeley described the town as being "a country where the regular administration of justice is yet a matter of prophecy." Courtesy, Colorado Historical Society

RIGHT: J. Bright Smith was another of Denver's pioneer lawyers, arriving in the area in October 1859. He served as city clerk and city attorney from 1861 until 1863. When there was another call for Colorado statehood in 1865, Smith was named candidate for Supreme Court justice, but the call proved to be 11 years premature. Courtesy, Colorado Historical Society

ABOVE: Like many of Denver's pioneers, Moses Hallett came to the region intent on discovering gold, but instead found more prosperity in Denver's business life. Hallett was appointed to the Colorado Territorial Supreme Court in 1866 after the Territorial Assembly asked President Andrew Johnson to appoint a local resident to the post, rather than one of the "carpetbaggers" who were flocking to the region. Courtesy, Colorado Historical Society

am entitled, if you will accord it to me?" The implication, at that time, was a challenge to duel. Harrison sent both letters to the *Rocky Mountain News.*

Several lawyers in town held a quick meeting about this publicized quarrel. Setting the precedent for years to come, this group of lawyers formed two committees: one to look at the dueling question, and one to look at organizing a more formal group of lawyers.

The next day, 16 members of the bar gathered at the offices of Mitchell Benedict and elected John W. Honer president and John Mechling secretary of their new bar association.

At that meeting, the group denounced dueling (or "the code of honor") as brutal, illegal, and unjust. The lawyers felt it was the professional duty of the bar to maintain law and order. The bar postponed formal incorporation of the association until a future meeting. The judicial significance of the courtroom battle between Harrison and Clough drifted away as quickly as it had appeared in the newspaper. But the lawyers of Denver—for the first time—had organized for a common purpose.

A Second Meeting: 1872

The first bar association was formed to resolve the dueling dispute and didn't have further meetings until January 4, 1872, in the rooms of the Probate Court. President Bela M. Hughes called the meeting to order and appointed C.W. Wright as secretary. Alfred Sayre, chairman of the committee on terms of court, reported that his committee unanimously proposed to reduce the terms of court. After discussion, this resolution was introduced:

Resolved. That it is the opinion of this meeting, that the probate court of Arapahoe County should have exclusive jurisdiction in all criminal matters arising in said county, saving and excepting cases of murder and manslaughter, and for that purpose said court should be a court of record.

After more discussion the Sayre resolution was passed, as was a second resolution offered by John Q. Charles:

Resolved. That we, as members of the bar of the city of Denver, are in favor of the enactment by the legislature of Colorado of a law limiting the terms of the probate court of this county to four, and limiting the number of terms of the district court to two.

The bar met again five days later with H.P.H. Bromwell presiding and David B. Graham recording. Judge Behlen, chairman of a committee on legislative issues, reported that the committee had prepared two bills for presentation to the legislature.

The first, "An act to regulate the jurisdiction of the probate court of Arapahoe County and for other purposes," provided "exclusive jurisdiction to the probate court over all indictable offenses except cases of treason, murder, and manslaughter; the appointment of a clerk to said court, for the empaneling and payment of grand and petit juries; for the certifying up of cases of treason, murder, and manslaughter, when the indictments are found in the probate court, into the district court; the payment of an annual salary of $3,000 for the probate judge; and for terms of courts and various practical reforms."

According to a newspaper account of the meeting, "a violent discussion ensued."

The second bill addressed changes of the judicial districts and the time of holding courts. This bill was presented concurrently with the first bill.

At the close of 1872, the *Rocky Mountain News* acknowledged the formal establishment of the Denver Bar Association and the ambitious purpose the small coalition of lawyers planned for their future.

Part of the editorial read:

LEFT: Throughout the mining regions of early Colorado, Miners' Courts were first established to judge the legality of mining claims and to fix the limits of the mining districts. Based on an idea that originated during the California Gold Rush of 1849, these courts were often the only form of government available in the camps. Courtesy, Denver Public Library, Western History Department

ABOVE: William N. Byers, founder of the Rocky Mountain Daily Evening News, *was one of early Denver's strongest boosters. In his editorials he encouraged Denver to change from a wild frontier town to one with an organized government, legal system, and established society. Courtesy, Colorado Historical Society*

. . . We are glad to note that the attorneys of this city have . . . taken the preliminary steps for the organization of a "Bar and Library association" . . . the object of the association is thus stated: To establish and maintain the honor and dignity of the profession of law; to cultivate social intercourse among its members; and to increase its usefulness in promoting the administration of justice; also to maintain a law library.

Let the aim of these organizations be to secure justice, not mere success, and the peace, good order, and welfare of the community will be conserved; the public morals preserved, and the profession of law rendered more honorable and more worthy of public confidence and respect, because it will become the right-hand assistant of justice and not the refuge to which criminals flee in the times of their merest tribulation. The Denver Bar Association, with its avowed objects, has our best wishes for success.

The establishment of this 1872 Denver Bar Association was attributed to General Bela M. Hughes, who practiced for more than 50 years in Denver. As Colorado became a territory, Hughes became the

manager of Holladay's Overland Stage Lines and served as the legal advisor for the company.

However, this bar association, for unknown reasons, faded into obscurity.

Denver Bar Association historian Edward Ring, in 1929, looked back on the pioneer times and said that the history of the Denver Bar fell naturally into two periods. The first, which began with the gold rush to Pike's Peak in 1859, was:

a formative and constructive era, in which the bench and bar were called upon to deal with new and significant questions. The development of mining and irrigation law led to sharp conflicts of personal rights, and raised issues for which there were no precedents; powerful railroads were fighting for rights of way through the mountain canyons and gorges; through legislative enactments and court decisions, unique and far-reaching principles were being crystallized into law.

He believed the second period, which started with the erection of the court house in 1881, was "less colorful."

Bar members now were trained in colleges and law schools, he pointed out, and a "natural result" from this followed:

In mental outlook, in habits of work and in personal appearance, lawyers reached a uniform level. They have become cogs in the business machinery of the community. The Denver Bar has its great lawyers—as great as those of the past—but the picturesque background of the earlier day has departed and with it the lawyer who was inevitably a prominent character and a fashioner of public opinion. The profession is now standardized.

A Time of Transition

Judicial proceedings in Denver soon hit rather shaky ground.

The *Rocky Mountain News* noted that when the September 1873 District Court began its three-month session, it cost the county at least $100 a day, during which no one tried a single civil suit. Demurrers and miscellaneous motions occupied two-thirds of the court's time; the other third was taken up by discussions of the merits of cases, apparently none of which reached trial. The *Rocky Mountain*

While awaiting trial for murder in 1860, the mayor of Leavenworth and a posse of 50 men were required to protect James A. Gordon from the angry citizens who were intent on seeing justice served. Although the Leavenworth city jail had only two cells during Gordon's incarceration, a new jail facility was constructed to alleviate the overcrowding of prisoners. The new facility is shown here in 1874. Courtesy, Kansas State Historical Society

ABOVE: Henry A. Clough began his Colorado law career as a clerk in the territorial district court. He was later appointed to the post of probate judge of Arapahoe County, and it was during his administration that the Probate Court assumed importance as a court of civil jurisdiction. Courtesy, Colorado Historical Society

RIGHT: Isaac N. Stevens achieved notoriety in the 1880s while working as district attorney for the Second Judicial District. He successfully prosecuted Dr. T. Thatcher Graves for poisoning one of his patients, a case which became a nationwide front page scandal. Stevens later became the editor of the Colorado Springs Gazette *and the author of three Progressive era novels. Courtesy, Denver Public Library, Western History Department*

News advocated the creation of a legislative commission to revise the town's laws.

The *News* challenged the Denver legal profession, claiming it was procrastinating in making the transition from common law to a more formal legal system of codes and statutes until Colorado achieved statehood. In Probate Court a discussion upon a demurrer on the point whether certain pleas should conclude "to the court" or "to the county" continued for two days. Under a code, the *News* editorialized, "courts should not spend a moment's time with such questions."

A New Attempt at Forming a Bar Association

On September 1, 1881, Isaac N. Stevens called to order a meeting of a new Denver Bar Association in Judge Richard Sopris' courtroom. Stevens explained that he thought an association with a large and flourishing membership could boost the morale of the legal profession in Denver through socialization and organization.

As Stevens explained, "It would also, if it adopted proper rules and regulations, offer a strong check to the practice of fraud and chicanery among members of the profession." He thought further, the *Rocky Mountain News* said, "that a large personal acquaintance would prevent the too great discourtesy often shown by members of the profession toward each other."

Alfred Sayre, in practice in Denver for more than 25 years, was an ardent promoter of the establishment of a bar association. He cited the unprofessional behavior of some lawyers who were unfaithful to their clients or guilty of fraud. Sayre thought most of his peers were honorable and fair-minded, "but legal tricksters should be punished." With the creation of the proper rules and regulations and a standing peer-review committee, Sayre believed that the actions of the legal profession in Denver could be self-regulated.

After listening to comments from attending attorneys, the organizers proposed the establishment of the Denver Bar Association and a good law library. M.A. McDonald and Walter S. Sullivan served as president and secretary of the temporary organization. Sullivan and Isaac N. Stevens drafted a preamble or prospectus, and John P.

Heisler, A.B. Sullivan, and M.A. McDonald were appointed as a committee to solicit membership.

As before, the "objects in forming such an association are to elevate the dignity of the bar, to improve the social relations among the members of the legal profession and to raise the standard of legal ethics and advance the cause of legal literature."

The *Rocky Mountain News* reported:

As there are a large number of high-minded and honorable gentlemen in this city engaged in the legal profession, there has for many years been a feeling among them that there ought to be formed among them an association for the promotion of social intercourse among their members, for mutual improvement and for the suppression of unprofessinal and dishonorable acts by the fraternity. Movements looking towards this end have frequently failed, but a number of young attorneys have lately determined to go to work in earnest for the inauguration of a movement which shall include, if possible, all men of proper professional standing throughout the city, and which shall have such objects as will commend it to the honorable opinion of the public at large.

ABOVE: *Photographed during the 1864 Camp Weld Council, mountain man John Simpson Smith (back row, second from right) was one of Denver's first residents. A trader with the Cheyenne and Arapahoe tribes, Smith often served as an interpreter and became one of the Indians' greatest allies. Courtesy, Colorado Historical Society*

LEFT: *John P. Heisler arrived in Denver in 1870 with just enough cash to last him one week, but eventually he found work building one of the first railroads into town. In 1876 he became the first lawyer admitted to the newly created state bar, entered politics, and served in the state legislature. Heisler was also appointed to a committee to solicit membership for the third Denver Bar Association in 1881. Courtesy, Colorado Historical Society*

This Denver Bar Association was as short-lived as the previous organizations.

Again in 1887, F.T. Johnson, Robert Bonynge, and Robert Latta attempted to rekindle the bar association. The trio later went on to other professions— Johnson became a district judge, Bonynge went to Congress, and Latta turned to journalism. But their effort to form a permanent association of lawyers failed.

The need for a bar association, however, had not diminished.

A NEW BAR ASSOCIATION

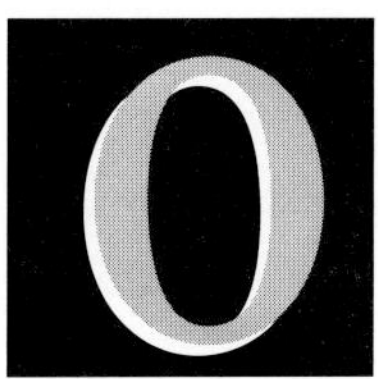

On Halloween evening in 1891, 125 of 159 available lawyers met at the Odd Fellows Hall, a landmark that still stands at 1545 Champa Street, to establish the Denver Bar Association, which still exists 100 years later.

This time the purpose of the organization was stated as follows:

To create a spirit of professional brotherhood, maintain a high ethical standard, throw around the practice of the law proper safeguards and restrictions, and therefore serve the best interests of the public. It holds every practitioner to strict responsibility for his conduct, guards his rights when unjustly assailed, and places character above wealth or fame.

Judge Moses Hallett gave the opening address and talked about the importance of lawyers' associations and how they functioned in other states. Citing the accomplishments of the National Bar Association, Judge Hallett explained how that organization was instrumental in creating a Court of Appeals.

Robert D. Thompson was elected temporary chairman and J.M. Lomery, temporary secretary. Once the official voting took place, A.E. Pattison emerged as the first president. He was succeeded in turn by George C. Norris, Thomas J. O'Donnell, Cass E. Herrington, W. Henry Smith, Charles D. Hayt, H.W. Bryant, and Hugh Butler. Vice president for the 1891 bar was William E. Beck; secretary was James M. Lomery; treasurer was Milton J. Stair, and sergeant-at-arms and doorkeeper was Ellery Stowell.

The first order of business was a long discussion over a motion to have a committee appointed to pass on the eligibility of future members. Newspaper accounts described the discussion as "witty and serious, philosophical and practical." On motion, all members present at the first bar association meeting were declared charter members.

The purpose of the new bar organization was to strengthen Denver's judicial system and to improve the public's perception of the bar.

As soon as the elegant Brown Palace Hotel opened in 1892 it became one of Denver's most prestigious hotels and has remained so for the past 100 years. The bar association chose the Brown Palace as the site for their first annual banquet in 1893. Courtesy, Colorado Historical Society

ABOVE: Judge Moses Hallett delivered the opening address at the October 31, 1891, meeting in which the Denver Bar Association was formed. The Denver Post *referred to Hallett as "a judicial trail blazer." Courtesy, Colorado Bar Association*

RIGHT: Pioneer lawyer Platt Rogers was one of seven lawyers who practiced law in Denver before 1874. Rogers was the first judge of the Criminal Division of the District Court and later earned the nickname "iron-handed" mayor during his mayoral term in the 1890s. Courtesy, Denver Public Library, Western History Department

By the close of 1900, membership increased to approximately 250 members. At last Denver had a bar association that gained the enthusiastic support of the legal profession.

The legal community in 1901 was a "conspicuously able one," according to comments by journalist Jerome Smiley:

The successful lawyer here must be a man of decided ability and of untiring industry. The practice covers a far wider range than in other parts of the country and, as indicated in the foregoing, encounters cases of extreme intricacy . . .The Denver lawyer must be a fighting lawyer if he expects to win; and his weapons must be those of learning, intelligent perceptions, of mental alertness, and original resources. He must, furthermore, expect and prepare to be met and opposed by another man as well equipped as he.

Some "longtimers" who practiced law during these pioneer times came to a bar association meeting in the 1920s to regale members with their stories. Seven lawyers who had practiced law since before 1874 included Platt Rogers (admitted 1873), George Q. Richmond (admitted 1871), D.B. Graham (admitted 1871), Herman E. Luthe (admitted 1872), Alfred C. Phelps (admitted 1872), E.A. Colburn (admitted 1873), and Webster Ballinger (admitted 1874).

Platt Rogers, mayor of Denver from 1891 to 1893, related that when he joined the bar, he knew virtually every attorney in the state, but at the time of the reunion, he said, there were 10 to 100 times as many attorneys.

He traced the origin of the practice acts upon which Denver attorneys based law. Lawyers used common-law practices while Colorado was a territory. The revised statutes of 1868 originated in a code written in New York in 1848. Attorneys who joined the Gold Rush to the west in 1849 carried it

to California where, with a few variations, it became known as the Parker Practice Act. As settlers sought more lucrative claims, they brought the judicial law with them to Montana and the Rocky Mountain region. Eventually Judge G.G. Symes brought the statutes to Colorado.

George Q. Richmond told of leaving the Union Army in 1865 and completing his law studies in Washington, D.C. He had the opportunity to listen to prominent legislators, jurists, and orators of the day.

Richmond arrived in Colorado in 1870 and became one of Denver's 143 practicing lawyers the following year. He told the members of the 1924 bar that 50 years earlier the legal system did not compromise with criminals. If the court charged a man with a crime, he went to court, pled not guilty, and told his story to the jury, or he pled guilty and confessed to the judge. There were no nolle contendere or technical guilty pleas that provided probation for the prisoner.

ABOVE: Vice president of the 1891 Denver Bar Association, William E. Beck served as a delegate to the state's Constitutional Convention, and later as a judge in the First Judicial District. He was selected for the state Supreme Court in 1880, where he served as chief justice for six years. Courtesy, Colorado Historical Society

LEFT: Hugh Butler emigrated to Central City from his native Scotland in 1863, and was elected mayor of that community just eight years later. Throughout his active political career, Butler also served in three territorial legislatures, was chairman of the state's Democratic party, and was a lecturer at the University of Colorado Law School in Denver. Courtesy, Denver Public Library, Western History Department

The Annual Meeting

While these gentlemen practiced law in Denver, the bar association began the colorful institution known as the annual meeting where "the shafts of fun and satire flew far and free."

On the evening of February 23, 1893, President George C. Norris, second president of the DBA, gave the command to fall in. Members who had been socializing on the eighth floor of the Brown Palace Hotel entered the banquet hall for the first annual dinner of the Denver Bar Association. Musicians performed soft-and-sweet strains of fine Italian music on harp and flute. After consuming 67 bottles of wine, the 104 members of the bar prepared their cigars.

President Norris addressed the association, explaining why there was a continuing need for a bar association. With the increase of renegade lawyers practicing in Denver and the unprofessional acts that abounded, the association would be representative of the most

ABOVE: Civil War veteran George G. Symes was responsible for introducing the Denver legal community to the practice arts upon which Denver attorneys based the law. He was elected to Congress in 1884 and 1886 and constructed the Symes Building at 16th and Champa Streets, which housed the Symes Law Library and which served as the site for several terms of the U.S. District Court. Courtesy, Colorado Historical Society

ABOVE, RIGHT: Active in Denver's legal community for many years, George Q. Richmond served as county attorney, city attorney, district attorney, appellate judge, and mayor. When he died in 1931 at the age of 91, he was the oldest practicing lawyer in the state. Courtesy, Colorado Historical Society

RIGHT: Charles D. Hayt left New York for the pioneer town of Alamosa in 1874. He held various judicial positions in Huerfano County before coming to Denver to sit on the state Supreme Court, where he eventually became chief justice in the 1890s. Courtesy, Denver Public Library, Western History Department

reputable members of the legal profession. Only through a strong and active association could the reputation of those in the profession remain intact.

According to a next-day account in the *Rocky Mountain Herald*, T.J. O'Donnell then introduced the first speaker of the evening, Colorado Supreme Court Justice Charles D. Hayt, Jr., who described upcoming changes in the administration of the Supreme Court. First, the legislature proposed to dispense with individually typeset printed records and abstracts. "Should the bill become a law," cautioned Hayt, "it will destroy all hope of progress. The typewriter serves a useful purpose, but the time has not yet arrived when it can supplant the printing press."

Hayt also described how the development of Denver as a city entering the twentieth century was causing delays in the judicial system:

Recently it took two weeks to secure a jury for the trial of a case in one of our district courts. Any person in this room could have selected a jury equally as able, and more impartial, in an hour. There is something radically wrong in a system which allows this . . . The modern system of stenographic reporting of trials is of doubtful benefit . . . We live in a progressive age. Conservatism must take a back seat on the bench and at the bar, and it behooves us as a profession to bring the practice of law abreast with the requirements of the present enlightened age.

"Retainers" was the subject of the next speaker, the Honorable Charle S. Thomas, governor of Colorado (1899-1901) and U.S. senator (1913-1921).

Retainers, he began, are to the profession what steam is to an engine. "It is as necessary to successful effort as the lever to the fulcrum."

Thomas then spoke about the bar association:

. . . there is a bond of genuine fraternity and good will among Denver attorneys which this association does much to increase. There is in Denver a spirit of fellowship which prompts courtesy and aids kindly feelings, which directs us older members of the bar to reach down and help the rising young man, and which ever urges us to think of others besides our own dear selves. Our purpose is to enhance the value and constancy of justice, to resist the oppressor, to preserve the integrity and righteousness of our profession and make the world better.

Among the new members of the Denver Bar Association was John Hipp, a champion of prohibition. When the bar planned the third annual meeting, Hipp moved to make the event dry. Another member concurred and recommended that additional speeches replace drinking. The banquet committee tabled the motion and the banquet continued in the "wet" tradition.

Advertising

The bar became concerned with an 1892 advertisement stating: "Legal advice furnished free; divorces obtained quickly, with no exposure." Declaring such advertisements as reprehensible, the more conservative members described the advertising lawyers as "harpies."

The bar appointed Judge J.B. Belford, S.P. Kose, and G.C. Norris to investigate the advertising attorneys. A few months later the association applauded this toned-down advertisement: "Divorces legally obtained very quietly. Good anywhere. Divorcees need not appear in court. Address Lawyer, 2107 Lawrence Street."

The committee scorned the trend toward advertising, insisting that divorce ads were "encouraging domestic wrangling." The bar threatened advertising attorneys with disbarment, but there is no record of any such action.

Briefs and Banquets

Toward the end of the century, the Denver Bar Association was growing. Membership had increased, and a permanent library in the courthouse made legal periodicals, magazines, and reports available to members of the legal profession.

The bar also scheduled six dinner meetings throughout the year, with attendance mandatory at least once.

George C. Norris was chosen as president of the Denver Bar Association in 1893, the same year the association established its first annual dinner banquet. He ran unsuccessfully for district judge on the People's Party ticket the following year. Norris later served the Denver community as a member of the Board of Public Works and as city attorney. Courtesy, Colorado Historical Society

Like many others in the nineteenth century, W. Henry Smith came to Colorado for the curative effects of its climate. Smith acted as prosecutor for the City of Denver in its unsuccessful suit against the Denver Union Water Company, which held a monopoly on the city's water supply, but he went on to establish a flourishing local practice. Courtesy, Colorado Historical Society

Practitioners, explained President Gustave C. Bartels in 1894, "must be present at the grace for the dinner, during the entire dinner, and until the concluding grace for the dinner. This rule, gentlemen, will be especially invoked this evening."

The Honorable Charles S. Thomas, first speaker of the evening for one dinner in 1894, challenged the members' knowledge of Latin with his subject, "Nulli Vendemus, Negabimus aut Difforemus, rectum vel Justitian," or, the impartial administration of justice.

The Honorable Henry C. Van Schaack followed with his talk on "Briefs and Banquets." He commented that a busy lawyer was saddled with the preparation of a brief. It was the judge, however, who was condemned to read it. Van Schaack continued:

In this respect, the judge has a decided advantage, for it has long since become an unwritten law with the judges of the appellate courts of Colorado that no member of the court is expected to read a brief, so that they all come to the hearing of a cause on a footing of perfect equality.

Bar banquets continued to be a forum of legal wit and professional encouragement, satirizing decisions made from the bench and the courtroom styles of the bar. By the eighth annual meeting, in 1900, the affairs had become familiar social activities.

At that meeting, Judge Morton S. Bailey spoke on "Merger in Law and Politics," noting that in the past many good lawyers made mighty poor state officials, thus wasting their education. Other speakers rose to address the political events of 1900.

Charles W. Franklin presented an analysis of the gambling casinos and bawdy houses of Denver's lower downtown district:

My good pastor had accomplished the feat of disclosing nine gambling houses in 36 minutes. I was told that the secret would never have been divulged had it not been that a lonesome and discouraged citizen had wandered into a gambling dive and made a winning—the shock killed him.

He described the legal battle to stop gambling in Denver as "the costliest litigation currently being addressed in the courts."

The speeches dragged on until 1 a.m. and the *Denver Post* reported that the banquet had "opened with good spirits and closed with better ones."

Before the 1906 bar banquet, in which attendees had to pay for alcoholic beverages and cigars, one disgruntled barrister told the newspaper, "There is but one thing to do, and that is to stay away. I know of at least 50 prominent attorneys who will not attend the banquet . . . The idea of abandoning the wine and cigars is about the fiercest thing I ever heard of."

During the 1906 banquet, the tone changed from one of merriment to one of bitter feelings and resentment.

Attorney H.N. Hawkins of Patterson, Richardson & Hawkins, counsel for the men charged with attempting to assassinate Supreme Court Justice Luther M. Goddard with a bomb, rose during the banquet to make light of the matter. Hawkins stated that his clients had left the state, and that "the only kind of bombs you'll ever hear explode will be the popping of champagne corks."

Justice Goddard, "pale and cool," who had been in the best of spirits at the banquet, rose without humor to point out "I have been walking in the path of death for eighteen months and doing my duty and if you can see anything humorous in it, I can't."

He also said to Hawkins and the rest of the bar:

A member of the bar has a right to defend an assassin, but when a lawyer jokingly refers to the planting of ten pounds of dynamite under a man's gate for the purpose of blowing him into eternity, I think no more of that lawyer than I do of the assassin . . . Any man who holds the position of judge ought to feel that he can decide questions that come before him after the dictates of his own conscience.

The next morning Justice Goddard clarified the statements he made at the banquet:

I did not say, neither did I insinuate, that any lawyer did not have the right to defend his client upon any charge; that is not only the right of a lawyer, but his solemn duty to defend any who may apply to him . . . the right of defense by counsel is one of our most sacred rights, and no man in these days of civilization should be denied the right of counsel under any circumstances or conditions.

The question of prohibition remained a controversial one. Attorney

In 1892 the Denver Bar Association debated the propriety of advertising legal services. Much scorned and threatened with disbarment, advertising attorneys soon learned to temper their often brash promotions. Some 19 years earlier three law firms (and one liquor dealer) had listed their services in the city directory. Courtesy, Colorado Historical Society

In 1860 Denver's largest library held a total of 14 volumes. Some 16 years later, however, the first state legislature approved the creation of a Supreme Court library to be located in the Capitol building. Shown here in the early 1900s, the State Capitol library served the needs of the Denver legal community for many years. Courtesy, Denver Public Library, Western History Department

John Hipp (previously mentioned as a staunch prohibitionist) remained quiet about the liquor served at bar association meetings. However, in 1908 he noted that the association's treasury continued to show a deficit due to the excessive expense for wine. He proposed celebrants should pay for their own wine. Despite Hipp's protest, the board referred his motion to a committee chaired by W. W. Garwood. Attorney John Gabriel, known as a peacemaker, poured oil on the troubled waters and suggested that the association not pay for any liquor at banquets. He did propose guests could bring their own. The motion passed.

Changes in Procedure

By 1912 "insurgency was rampant" within the Denver Bar Association, according to the *Denver Post.* "Young, progressive lawyers" had secured control of the organization.

In the past it was the custom of the president to appoint all standing committees for the year. Inspired by a recent coup in Congress where insurgents named the rules committee from the floor, these "insurgents" in the Denver Bar railroaded through a new bylaw that let the general membership elect a judiciary committee of five which would observe the workings of the judicial system (a "sort of espionage," according to some of the more stalwart conservative members). They would also consider the fitness of candidates for election or appointment to the bench or to any office connected with the administration of justice.

They also proposed to cut out the "undesirables" in the profession. In the past only members of the association could present complaints to the grievance committee. Under the new bylaw anyone could bring charges of misconduct against any member of the bar and secure a trial of the offending attorney.

Other radical changes in the bar administration enabled 15 members of the bar to petition the association to call a special meeting to address quick action on pertinent issues. To encourage new blood within the organization, the bar halted the automatic succession of vice president to president. Individual officers would have to stand on their own merits during elections.

The first assignment of the bar president's committee was to select judges for the district bench of the Second Judicial District. The 750-member roster of the Denver Bar Association comprised the list of potential nominees. The first election occurred on June 28, 1912, in the safety vault rooms of the Equitable Building, still standing at 17th and Stout. The membership voted for five candidates, and the judicial committee served as election judges.

A bar association spokesman told the press:

It is the opinion of members of the bar that the selections of today's voting will represent the best possible candidates, and that lawyers are better able to judge the qualifications of a candidate for district judge than is the layman. It is also the belief that the candidates selected by them will be non-partisan in every sense of the word and thereby removed from corrupt political influence and party favoritism.

This drawing, which depicts the early hours of the Denver Bar Association banquet of February 24, 1900, appeared in the Denver Post *with an accompanying article. Many issues of the day were debated at these annual affairs, offering association members the opportunity to both socialize and discuss the concerns of the legal community. Courtesy, Colorado Historical Society*

Bonfils and Tammen Attack Judiciary

The candidate selection process, with attorneys selecting judicial candidates, came under immediate fire when district judge (and candidate) Hubert L. Shattuck found himself in the middle of an affray between the *Denver Post* and the *Denver Times.*

The *Post*'s founders, Harry H. Tammen and Fred G. Bonfils, were always in the middle of a controversy. When the voters allowed William G. Evans to receive the franchise of the Tramway Company, the *Post* pundits began, on May 18, 1912, to editorially vent their spleen on everyone associated with the election.

Evans was caught in the middle of their tirades and promptly sued the newspapermen for libel.

At that point, the enraged editors of the *Post* wrote so many editorial comments against the judiciary that Judge Hubert L. Shattuck named a committee consisting of former Supreme Court Justice Julius C. Gunter, former Mayor Platt Rogers, and Attorney Caldwell Yeaman to consider citing Tammen and Bonfils for criminal contempt. The definition of criminal contempt was "holding the court up to public ridicule or scorn, of attacking the integrity and honor of the court and of endeavoring to influence, by coercion or intimidation, the rulings and decisions of the court in a case on trial or about to come to trial."

At issue were editions of the *Denver Post* published July 8-9 and 11-12, which the prosecution claimed were "contemptuous and tending to disparage the honor and integrity of the court and designed to arouse public sentiment and to coerce and intimidate the court." Bonfils' July 9th editorial, "So the People May Know," particularly singled out the bar association:

WHAT EVERYBODY KNOWS—There is a Bar association in Denver, composed of almost all the lawyers, but it seems to be a sleeping association, and it

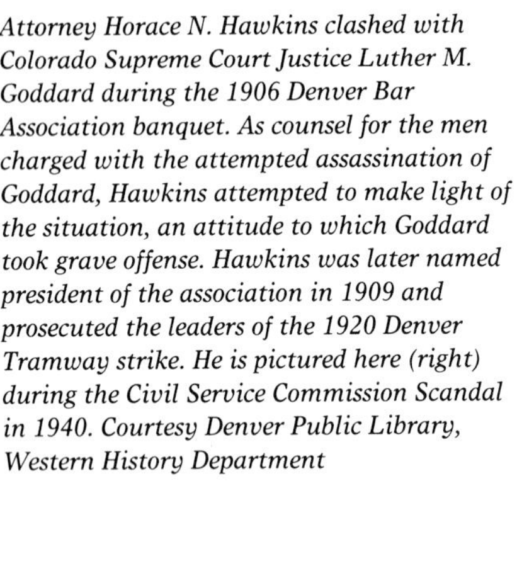

Attorney Horace N. Hawkins clashed with Colorado Supreme Court Justice Luther M. Goddard during the 1906 Denver Bar Association banquet. As counsel for the men charged with the attempted assassination of Goddard, Hawkins attempted to make light of the situation, an attitude to which Goddard took grave offense. Hawkins was later named president of the association in 1909 and prosecuted the leaders of the 1920 Denver Tramway strike. He is pictured here (right) during the Civil Service Commission Scandal in 1940. Courtesy Denver Public Library, Western History Department

would be hard to guess what would be necessary to awaken it. We wonder if the only object of this association is to pass resolutions on departed members and meet occasionally, smoke and swap lies, and if the association has no higher aims than this.

What do you lawyers, you men who practice before our courts, think of the Colorado judges? . . . Isn't it true that there are judges in our local district courts who hold their positions as judges due entirely to the influence of their corporation friends? Don't you lawyers know this? And can't you all pick out who these judges are by the decisions they render and by their deportment on the bench? . . . Isn't it about time that you lawyers and your Bar association took some public steps to clean out our corporation-ridden and controlled district bench?

There are, of course, some honest men among the district judges—the people know who they are and also know who the corporation judges and tools are. Isn't it time that we should begin local impeachment against corrupt judges, as has been commenced against Judge Archibald, a United States judge who has disgraced his calling, his country and his family?

Supreme Court Justice Luther M. Goddard concurred in a decision declaring the eight-hour workday law unconstitutional in the early 1900s. As a result of this opinion, he found himself the object of an unsuccessful assassination attempt by certain members of the Western Federation of Miners. Courtesy, Denver Public Library, Western History Department

Judge Shattuck prepared to evaluate the contempt of court charges, but discharged the committee five days later. He appointed a committee of lawyers, then appointed Deputy District Attorney John Horne Chiles to consider contempt charges. Shattuck instructed Chiles to "prosecute vigorously anyone shown to be guilty of contempt of court."

On July 25, 1912, Fred G. Bonfils' criminal contempt trial began in the Westside court before Judge Shattuck and Special Prosecutor John Horne Chiles. Bonfils maintained that his published reports, protected under the First Amendment, were not contemptuous or intended to influence the court. Through his attorney, Bonfils pled "lack of interest to attack the honor, integrity and dignity of the court and that he was compelled in self-defense to publish the editorials and news matter in question."

During the spirited court trial, Attorney John T. Bottom, counsel for Bonfils, read one article published in the *Post*. In the section pertaining to the selection of judicial candidates by the DBA, he said there was nothing contemptuous about the comments. Bottom declared that the term "pinhead" in one of the articles certainly did not refer to Judge Shattuck, but, rather, that it might be "applicable to at least one or two other judges on the district bench."

When the court offered Bonfils an opportunity to correct any misunderstandings caused by the editorials, the publisher said:

I haven't now, and never have had anything but the kindest feeling and best wishes for this court. I wish it were in my power to make your honor the most righteous judge that ever blessed a struggling people . . . that you might teach the world the beneficence and wisdom of the Master, and that through you and your rulings we might all learn to do unto others as we would have others do unto us; and that your honor's decisions might hasten the final redemption and salvation of all mankind—because I know of no community that so badly needs such a judge.

The next day the court found Bonfils guilty of contempt of court.

He was sentenced to 60 days in the county jail and fined $5,000 and half the court costs. Judge Shattuck called the convicted Bonfils to the bench and started to hand him one of the Bibles he traditionally presented to convicted criminals or offenders.

"Take this to jail with you and read it," the judge said.

"I refuse to take it," replied Bonfils, turning his back on the judge and taking his seat at counsel's table. Bonfils later reported that he refused the Bible because he did not want "to take any part in a sacrilegious burlesque of that kind."

Harry H. Tammen left Denver in the middle of the night on a month-long vacation in Honolulu the same night that Judge Shattuck issued a bench warrant charging him with criminal contempt of court.

For weeks Bonfils ranted and raved on the front pages of the *Denver Post*. He wanted the recall of judges as a means to "crush corporation ownership of the courts." In another edition of the paper, he called judges "sacred oxen—you can't discharge them, you can't even criticize them—Hired by you, they are your masters."

When Tammen returned from vacation, he appeared before Judge Shattuck and listened to the charges.

Just before the judge passed sentence, Tammen jumped up, spun the podium away, and shook his fist at the startled judge. "Look here, Judge Shattuck, you know and I know that this is nothing but a cat and dog fight. You can put me in that jail for 20 years, if you want, but I'll get you yet!" The judge stared at the tyrannical publisher. "Case dismissed," the judge responded huskily.

Neither Tammen nor Bonfils ever did time for their charges against the Denver courts.

Bar Activities, 1913-1919

Members of the Denver Bar were talking about reform. In 1913 the association, according to the *Denver Post*, discussed reforms in pleading and practice and went over the changes in the District Court procedure: "They find in their way, at present, statutes which prohibit them from making rules which they desire. In order to reform the practice they will have to get the legislature to repeal certain old laws and make other new ones."

A meeting was called at the request of the judiciary committee on July 1, 1914, to consider a suggested amendment to a new rule of practice promulgated by the Supreme Court. The system of letting any lawyer issue a summons personally would be abolished and a provision substituted where the clerk of the court would issue summons only after the complaint had been filed.

The judiciary committee objected to abolishing this privilege, and so tried to put an amendment to the new rule which would continue the practice while "purporting to consent to the spirit of the new rule."

Judge Hubert Shattuck, who presided at the libel trial of Frederick G. Bonfils and Harry H. Tammen in 1912, was one of Denver's most respected judges in the late 1800s and early 1900s. Even so, he understood the lasting power of the press and eventually dismissed the case when Tammen threatened personal retribution. Courtesy, Colorado Historical Society

The new rule is salutary, timely and altogether admirable. The only men with real objections to it are the jack-leg lawyers who have used the old method for blackmailing purposes or for worrying poor and ignorant people into the payment of debts for which they may not have been legally responsible . . . We are weeding out black-legs and shysters and this new rule of the supreme court will accelerate the process most happily.

Co-founder of the Denver Post, *Frederick G. Bonfils styled himself as Denver's great crusader for the common people and titled his* Post *editorials "So the People May Know." He was once shot by a lawyer as the result of a money dispute, following his successful campaign to get cannibal Alferd Packer paroled. Bonfils was also active in the libel feud between the newspaper and William G. Evans, after Evans was granted the Tramway Company franchise by voters in 1912. Courtesy, Denver Public Library, Western History Department*

However, the association meeting resulted in the adoption of a resolution asking the Supreme Court to amend the new rule.

During the 1916 annual meeting, the Denver Bar Association unanimously issued a declaration of independence from all political parties. One member pointed out that four years previously, the bar had nominated candidates for the district bench and "all of those candidates were elected." But, he added, "this year not one of our candidates was elected, because our influence was scattered."

Members of the bar decided by a unanimous vote not only to continue its system of nominating candidates for judicial offices at established bar primaries, but "to nominate by petition candidates so selected and thereby place them on the regular ballot whenever the political assemblies refuse to endorse such candidates."

Explained one lawyer:

Let us hold our bar primaries and vote for the candidates best qualified by experience, learning and character to fill vacancies. Let us vote in the public interest and, not to please a friend or punish an enemy . . . If the voters feel that we are working in the public interests and not in our personal interests and not to further the ends of some political party, the candidates of the Denver bar association will be elected.

Working with and for the judiciary would continue to be a major theme in bar association activities.

This final and permanent bar association was well on its way by 1920, almost 30 years after it was formed. The *Record,* published monthly by the Denver Bar, printed a story on law office management and mentioned the use of new filing cabinets, dictaphones and typewriters, and "proper office equipment and coordination of office work." A "Committee on Women and Children" existed.

And, of course, they were already starting to talk about the good old days—those "golden days" of lawyering when the practice was more challenging and more enjoyable.

Bartender, con man, entrepreneur, circus owner, and publisher, Harry H. Tammen was one of Denver's most colorful figures. Tammen and Frederick G. Bonfils purchased the failing Post *in 1895, and soon turned it into the most popular newspaper in town. Tammen is pictured here in the early 1900s. Courtesy, Denver Public Library, Western History Department*

LEGAL GIANTS

awyers love to talk about the good old days, and when two or more are gathered, they almost always do. It's hard to exactly pinpoint when these much-lauded golden years occurred. Actually, the only rule is that they can't be right now.

From the very first written record of the Denver Bar Association, lawyers were looking back: to the 1800s and times of riding the circuit, pitching camp with fellow lawyers outside of town; to the "rough and tumble" courts of the 1920s, where juries were pulled off the street; to the 1940s and 1950s, before oppressive depositions and super technology took away some of the fun and independence.

But mostly, when lawyers talk about the glory days, they remember the giants of the profession.

Young lawyers crowded courtrooms when these men went to trial. The great men were revered for their persuasive arguments to judge and jury, for their eloquence and sharp wit, sometimes for their audacity, and always for their character that seemed larger than life.

Gleaned from some early Denver Bar Association records and newspaper accounts are profiles of some of these leaders—they tell about the man and they tell something of the times in which they practiced.

In the pioneer days of the mid- to late 1800s, the name of **General Sam E. Browne** stands out. He was "a patriarchal figure in black Prince Albert coat, high hat, smooth shaven upper lip and long white beard. The old gentleman was geniality personified. His moral obliquities were obvious, his disregard of professional proprieties was notorious but his personality was irresistible." Browne practiced law for 40 years in Colorado. Later someone said of him: "In many respects he was a typical pioneer lawyer; democratic in his associations, liberal in his expenditures, catholic in his opinions and careless in his own business."

At about the same time, one lawyer paid tribute to **Judge Amos Steck,** who came seeking gold and stayed to practice law. Steck was described as a man who "swore when other men prayed, sang revival songs

As the population of Denver boomed around the turn of the century, so did the number of new lawyers. By 1912 the Denver Bar Association was being split along generational lines, and the younger and more progressive lawyers were gaining control of the group. Courtesy, Denver Public Library, Western History Department

From left to right, Justice of the Peace John S. Dormer, Jacob Downing, former Territorial Governor John Evans, and an unidentified companion stand outside of Dormer's Larimer Street office circa 1890. Downing quit his Denver law practice in order to lead the Colorado Cavalry in the Civil War, but later returned to Denver where he served as a probate judge. Courtesy, Denver Public Library, Western History Department

Pictured here in this circa 1880 portrait, Samuel H. Elbert, a member of the Nebraska legislature, was chosen by President Abraham Lincoln to act as secretary of the Colorado Territory. He remained active in Colorado politics, serving as a member of the Territorial Legislature, territorial governor, and Supreme Court justice. His name lives on in the form of Mount Elbert, the state's highest peak. Courtesy, Colorado Historical Society

when playing billiards, who never forgot a fact or a face, whose integrity was his obsession, and who feared no man." Steck was, for many years, judge of the Probate and County Court.

Then there was **Mayor Edmond L. Smith,** a "great outstanding common law lawyer. He selected his work, limiting it to his estimates of his own capacity and drunk or sober, was always ready and prepared. He was at all times the gentleman, never personal, caustic nor boisterous, seldom yielding to emotion, never dramatic, always earnest, luminous in expression and simple in speech."

One writer paid homage to other great lawyers of that time: "**Judge Markham**, the best equity lawyer of the territory; **Judge George W. Miller,** so ungainly and so homely as to be handsome; the stately and dignified **Gov. Elbert**; **Col. R.S. Morrison,** as quaint as he was capable; **Orris Blake,** whom I loved because he was taller and skinnier than I was; and old **Ham Hunt,** the perfect type of a lawyer frontiersman; **Mitchell Benedict,** big-framed, big-hearted, red-headed and jovial always, whose laugh was spontaneous, easily provoked and easily heard for a quarter of a mile. And there were **the Tellers, Hugh Butler, Thomas Macon, Cal**

Thatcher, and **W.G. Gorsline**, all giants in those days, and **Belford**, the red-headed rooster of the Rockies, graceful of speech, too impulsive to be judicial and too fond of politics to take root in the profession, obsessed with the notion that he was created for the bench and not for the forum."

Senator Charles Thomas remembered coming west to Denver with a letter of introduction to a lawyer who scowled at the idea of another lawyer setting up practice. The lawyer told the young Thomas to come back in the afternoon to see his partner. He would be easy to find, he said: "He looks like Napoleon and keeps an owl on his desk." Thomas stayed to practice and remembered Denver in the 1870s as having a population of about 8,000. Law offices were, for the most part, on Market and Larimer streets. One could count only a half-dozen houses between Broadway, then nothing but a country road, and Cheesman Park, then the city's cemetery.

Philadelphia lawyer Amos Steck went to California during the Gold Rush of 1849. Not finding any luck as a prospector, he made his way back to Denver where he began a long career of public service. Steck served as mayor, postmaster, member of the Territorial Council, and finally Supreme Court justice during his active career. Courtesy, Colorado Historical Society

Trials were often in front of **Judge Moses Hallett**, who was, on the bench, "the august personification of dignity." He was one of three territorial judges when Colorado became a state (and was appointed three times chief justice) and was later judge of the United States District Court. He was president of the Colorado Bar Association in 1900 and first dean of the Colorado University Law School. According to the *Denver Post,* upon his death in 1913 he was "the most famous mining judge Colorado ever has known. He was a judicial trail blazer and did more to establish the reign of law in the mining camps in the 1870s than any other agency."

At the turn of the century, **Thomas J. O'Donnell** "stood easily in the front rank

Vincent D. Markham had just finished a term in the Kansas legislature when he arrived in Denver on foot in 1862. He was later chosen as Arapahoe County attorney, and prosecuting attorney for the First Judicial District. He was probably better known, however, for owning the Markham Hotel, one of Denver's finest nineteenth-century establishments. Courtesy, Denver Public Library, Western History Department

After serving in the Civil War, Mitchel Benedict relocated to Denver, where he set up a thriving law practice. For his first case in Colorado he defended a wealthy rancher, and it was said that the fee he received was the basis of his considerable fortune. Benedict was instrumental in the establishment of the first Denver Bar Association in 1871. Courtesy, Colorado Historical Society

of good lawyers." A newspaper described him as "one of the strongest personalities in this state of strong men." He reminded one writer of a "knight in the days of old, riding against his adversary when the herald's trumpet sounded . . . He always charged with uplifted lance and battle-axe. When he died there fell a giant oak in Denver's legal timber." His briefs were replete with quotations from the great masters of the law, and from the greatest works of prose and poetry, despite his lack of formal education. He was also said to possess "the greatest denunciatory and invective vocabulary of any man I ever knew. He never let an insult pass unresented." He was said to be strong as an enemy, strong as a friend, working uncompensated in many cases for poor women or a "man unjustly dealt with." O'Donnell was president of both the Denver and Colorado **Bar Associations**.

Another man of this era, who went on to become a famous trial lawyer, was **Edward O. Wolcott**. He first began to practice in 1876. At his first jury trial, however, he suffered a severe case **of stage fright. A friend** commented: "He told me shortly afterwards that he never knew, nor ever would know, what he said to the jury, not a man of whom he could see, but he must have said something for he was conscious of making a protracted noise." (Wolcott won the case.) Someone commented later that in the history of the early bar "Wolcott was its great orator, Patterson its great gladiator and Hallett its great character."

A scribe of the modern bar association, Phil Dufford, said that law students in the 1930s, 1940s, and 1950s learned, almost as a litany, the names and famous trials of the giants of the Denver trial bar. "They were trial lawyers of the old style, back before federal rules. It was really trial by surprise."

Some of those names included:

Philip Hornbein, trial lawyer and persuasive orator who crusaded against the Ku Klux Klan in the 1920s and led the fight against Prohibition at the 1932 Democratic convention;

Kenneth Robinson, a superb trial attorney who had a vocabulary to match his rumbling voice;

Philip Van Cise, district attorney and trial lawyer known for smashing a million-dollar bunco ring, for his fight against the KKK, and the fact that he defended the *Rocky Mountain News* in a libel suit brought by *Denver Post* owner Fred Bonfils;

Horace Hawkins, legal scholar, trial attorney, and lecturer at Westminster (later DU) Law School;

Fred Dickerson, a larger-than-life criminal defense lawyer known for his intimidating cross examinations;

Ralph Carr, two-term Colorado governor who spoke out in behalf of persecuted Americans of Japanese origin during World War II;

William Lee Knous, Colorado governor, chief justice of the Colorado Supreme Court, and federal judge;

Warwick Downing, a conservationist who was called father of Denver's boulevards, playgrounds, and mountain parks;

Robert W. Steele, chief justice of the Colorado Supreme Court at the turn of the century and champion of individual rights;

Robert W. Steele, Jr., a Denver district judge for 38, years considered "dean of the Denver Bench";

Mary Lathrop, first woman member of the Denver Bar Association

Anthony F. Zarlengo received his law degree in 1928 and became assistant prosecutor in the Justice of the Peace Court. He was recently honored with a "roast" at the University Club attended by about 90 Denver Bar Association members over the age of 65. Courtesy, Colorado Bar Association

Pictured here at his desk circa 1930, Charles S. Thomas was named city attorney of Denver when he was just 26 years old. He ran unsuccessfully for Congress in 1884, but was elected governor of Colorado in 1899. Courtesy, Denver Public Library, Western History Department

Seen here in his office in the Peoples' Bank Building in the late 1800s, Alfred J. O'Brien was one of the most prominent lawyers in turn-of-the-century Denver. He was generally considered to be Colorado's foremost patent attorney. Courtesy, Denver Public Library, Western History Department

and one of two women to first join the American Bar Association, who was active in promoting legislation improving the status of women and children and had a 55-year legal career;

Max Melville, teacher, author, special prosecutor, called "Mr. Law."

"They were legends," Dufford said.

In recent years, Dufford interviewed many of the luminaries of the bar, some born right after the turn of the century. Here follows brief comments about some of them.

Anthony F. Zarlengo remembers the rough and tumble court of the late 1920s. "The courtrooms were always crowded. It was a form of entertainment for a lot of people and we were under a lot of pressure." Zarlengo's father was an Italian immigrant with a fourth-grade education. Zarlengo became an assistant prosecutor in the Justice of the Peace Court. At that time juries were just pulled off the street and many of the cases had to do with prohibition. Zarlengo (and many others)

Benjamin B. Lindsey was an internationally known legal reformer who made Denver's Juvenile Court one of the nation's best. The "Kids' Judge" later turned his attention to eliminating corruption in Denver's political machine. This muckraking gained Lindsey so many enemies that he was eventually disbarred in Colorado. Courtesy, Denver Public Library, Western History Department

treasure the independence they had and the responsibility—a lawyer took a case from beginning to end and had to learn to think quickly. Zarlengo got his law degree from Westminster in 1928: "All I wanted to do was be a trial lawyer."

John Gorsuch (founding partner of Gorsuch, Kirgis, Campbell, Walker & Grover, and president of the Denver Bar Association in 1946) remembered the joy and excitement of being a lawyer. "You just never knew what was going to walk in the door." After he received his law degree in 1925, his first job paid $50 per month. His real joy, he said, came from dealing with people and trying to solve their problems.

Samuel Sherman, Jr. (a prominent partner of Sherman & Howard), worked as a police reporter for the *Rocky Mountain News* before becoming a lawyer and attended Westminster law school when it was over the Mapelli Bros. Meat Market. He recalled fellow student Pete Silverstein (later chief judge of the Colorado Court of Appeals) taking friends home after class where they talked long and late about the law. Evenings usually ended with Harry S. Silverstein, Sr. (a prominent Denver lawyer), opening some home-bottled beer which had to be covered with a towel to avoid spraying the walls of their home. Sherman entered practice in 1935.

Glory days for **Louis G. Isaacson** (founding partner of his firm) were the days he fought for his clients as a sole practitioner. Graduating from the University of Chicago Law School, he began practicing in the 1930s:

Attorney Thomas J. O'Donnell was one of the most powerful members of the state's Democratic party in the 1890s. He was a foe of Frederick G. Bonfils, owner of the Denver Post, *and was once charged with assault with intent to kill as a result of a fistfight between the two on the steps of the Arapahoe County Court House. O'Donnell is depicted in this early 1900s cartoon. Courtesy, Colorado Historical Society*

"I was a one man band, doing everything. But it was the trial work that was fun. It was the happiest time of my life." He liked staying with a case all the way through, and knowing all those associated with the case.

Larry Long, born in 1908 and founding partner of his firm, remembers that his first job paid $75 a month ("very good for depression days") and that usually he was called "hey, you." Back then, he said, "justice was a faster, more definitive thing."

Others Dufford interviewed included **Noah Atler**, who was still putting in a full day at the office and teaching seminars in real estate law at age 84; "successful rebel" **Stephen H. Hart,** founding partner of Holland & Hart; **Churchill Owen**, a longtime partner in Holme Roberts & Owen and senior advisor to legions of lawyers; **Charles Beise**, who began practicing in the 1930s and later argued major water cases before the U.S. Supreme Court; **Donald S. Stubbs,** a senior partner of Davis, Graham & Stubbs who did much of his firm's trial work; **Ira Rothgerber, Jr.,**

The bigotry and violent racism of the Ku Klux Klan briefly found a wide audience in Denver in the 1920s. Klan support became crucial for politicians, while Ben Lindsey, who was the object of many Klan attacks, saw his Colorado career end during the Klan's brief reign of power. Courtesy, Denver Public Library, Western History Department

LEFT: Ralph Carr, who specialized in water and irrigation law, served as Colorado's governor from 1939 until 1943. He gained a national reputation in the Republican party and stood firm in his defense against the relocation of Japanese-Americans during World War II. It was rumored that Carr was in line to be Wendell Wilkie's running mate in the 1940 presidential election. Courtesy, Colorado Historical Society

FAR LEFT: Among other legal concerns of the day, the 1950s saw the Denver Bar Association successfully battle Colorado's real estate brokers and title insurance companies in the unauthorized practice of preparing deeds and other real estate contracts. Royal Rubright of the firm Fairfield and Woods was photographed in 1957 with the honorary gavel that was presented each year to the newly instated association president. Courtesy, Royal Rubright

who joined his father's firm (the oldest law firm of continuous existence in Denver) and was known as a philanthropist and excellent legal scholar; **Judge William E. Doyle**, prosecutor, private practitioner and Colorado Supreme Court justice and judge of both the U.S. District Court and the Court of Appeals for the Tenth Circuit (where "landmark cases flowed from his pen").

Other greats include U.S. District **Judge Alfred A. Arraj**, revered for his devotion to law and scholarship, and Colorado's own legendary athlete and outstanding justice of the U.S. Supreme Court, **Byron White**.

To Phil Dufford, the 1950s were the golden years. He remembers being in a four-person firm (about average in those days). He'd pick up a newspaper for a nickel, board the rubber-tired trolley, and read his paper in quiet comfort. He went to work early, often as the sun was coming up, because young lawyers worked long hours. At work, he could open windows to catch a sweet breeze. When lawyers went to court, it was to the majestic rooms of the federal court in the old Post Office or the spaciousness of original courtrooms in the City and County Building, where judges seemed to know every lawyer who came before them. Trial, if it came, came quickly. Some of the giants then included **Bill Dwyer, Erskine Myer, Fred Winner, George Creamer, Jim Bromley, and Bob Charlton**.

In the 1950s, Dufford said, lawyers cut their teeth examining abstracts, learning Denver's history. There was a closeness of space that encouraged the exchange of ideas between lawyers. The young ones making $150 a month packed brown bags, often lunching together and talking. "You didn't need a letter stipulation on an extension of time or a written receipt for a file from a lawyer you shared lunches with," he pointed out.

As the old buildings were torn down and new firms took space in the huge high rises, "we lost our simplicity and candor."

He especially treasures the memory of leaning out a third-floor law office window on 17th Street, on a balmy May day, watching and hearing birds and seeing the distinguished and elderly Warwick Downing jaywalk to the Albany Hotel without any concern about stop lights and traffic. ("He thought traffic lights were for other people.")

Probably every lawyer who ever reminisced about the better days that came before would agree with the sentiment of Senator Charles S. Thomas in his "old timer's speech" in 1924:

"My spirit is that of the older time and my memory dwells instinctively among the scenes and the events of vanished yesterdays. Their associations are the warp and the woof of my existence and I would not have it otherwise."

Mayor Speer's "City Beautiful" movement included the construction of Denver's new Civic Center. Work on the City and County Building began in 1924 and was completed in 1932. Pictured here in the late 1930s, the building housed a variety of government offices in addition to district, juvenile, and county courts. Courtesy, Denver Public Library, Western History Department

Mary Lathrop

It's often mentioned that Mary Lathrop, one of the first women to practice law in Colorado, was small in stature.

A friend recalled her tiny, stooped, white-haired figure as she walked to court, with "long, almost but not quite, trailing skirts, button shoes, unbelievable hats and an old black oilcloth shopping bag she used in lieu of a briefcase."

Her size, though, had nothing to do with her spirit.

Born in Philadelphia in 1865, the only child of well-educated Quaker parents of independent spirit, she was educated at girls schools. After her father died and their assets dissolved in a bank failure, it became essential that Mary earn a living for herself and her mother. She sold free-lance articles to the Philadelphia press, then was hired by the McClure Syndicate and sent far and wide to cover stories for its publications. For instance, during rioting in a mining camp in Cripple Creek, Colorado, troublemakers threatened to lynch any newspaperman found in the neighborhood. The McClure office sent Lathrop to cover the riots.

Why she moved to Colorado is not certain, but once here she enrolled at the University of Denver "against all advice." She graduated in 1896 and her grade on the bar exam was 96, the highest ever attained at that time. She went back to Philadelphia and studied probate law, then returned to Colorado in 1898, taking an office in the Equitable Building. She was the first woman admitted to the Denver Bar Association.

"As a woman, I was an oddity in journalism," she said, "but I didn't meet with open opposition until I entered law."

She was told from the first she would fail. "I rented an office for $12 a month, furnished it with second-hand desks and chairs and decided to live on the bottom rung of the ladder so that if I fell off I wouldn't get hurt."

She won her first court case by default when opposing counsel announced: "I will not try a case with a woman lawyer." Others in the legal community dismissed her as "that damn woman" in the early

One of the first women to be admitted to the American Bar Association and the first woman elected to the Denver bar, former newspaperwoman Mary Lathrop graduated from the University of Denver Law School in 1896. She gained national attention with her 1898 federal court case against Francis C. Grable and went on to become a staunch defender of legal reform and the rights of women and children. Courtesy, Denver Public Library, Western History Department

years. However, Mary Lathrop stayed to practice law successfully for 55 years.

She was invited by the American Bar Association to join in 1901, but she turned them down, believing most members didn't really want her to join. She accepted a unanimous bid in 1918, becoming one of the first two women members.

Miss Lathrop worked mainly in probate and real estate law. She was outspoken and often militant and resented being called a woman lawyer. "I'm either a lawyer or I'm not," she would say. "Don't drag my being a woman into it."

One of her memorable cases involved the George W. Clayton will, in which $2.5 million was left to establish a college for orphan boys. The will was attacked by T.S. Clayton. The case, which was won by Lathrop in the first argument by a woman in front of the Colorado Supreme Court, resulted in the law of charitable bequests in Colorado.

She was active in the Denver Bar, chairing a committee on women and children. She attended conventions of the American Bar Association every year, and became quite famous for her exclusive

dinner parties at the annual meeting.

Back home she had dinner parties of another sort, for "my boys," who were being mobilized for World War II. She often set her table for 16 or 24 but sometimes holiday parties would gather 100 or so. Friends estimated she entertained some 14,000 in uniform during her lifetime. She helped many with financial aid and free legal services.

Mary Lathrop collected many honors before her death in 1951. She left behind valuable changes in Colorado's probate laws and her legend as a pioneering lawyer.

MEET
-A-
LAWYER

For The Public Good

The frontier lawyer who followed the wagon ruts across the Great Plains to try his fortune among the Colorado gold diggings carried something with him that wasn't visible in his pack or saddle bags.

He carried a special sense that as a lawyer he had to do more than simply make a living for himself. Because of his profession, there would be certain claims on him.

Stretching back more than 500 years, lawyers and judges in England and the United States had labored mightily to build a strong tradition of professional responsibility. They insisted that lawyers were obligated to take part in improving the system of justice, to help eliminate shady practices and shady practitioners, to make sure the poor had legal representation, and to devote some of their time and energy and skill "pro bono publico—for the public good."

These obligations have been expressed in statutes, codes, ethical rulings, well-recognized traditions, and informal understandings since the thirteenth century. The legal literature of codes and commentaries on codes was massive. Nearly every lawyer who served an apprenticeship at the bar before moving to Denver would have brushed up against the concept of professional responsibility and understood its significance.

If some lawyers ignored what they had learned or thumbed their noses at it, many who set up practice near Cherry Creek and the Platte took the concept seriously and put it to work. They designed a justice system and worked to strengthen the courts. They spoke out against chicanery and fought the lawyers who engaged in it. They sought to get better judges and fairer procedures. They gave help to people who couldn't afford to pay. And they contributed fully to the improvement of the territorial, state, and local governments and to all kinds of community enterprise.

The tradition of professional responsibility which these pioneer lawyers brought to Denver and planted in the new settlement has persisted throughout the history of the Denver bar.

As part of Law Week, Denver Bar Association lawyers answer legal questions on the 16th Street Mall. Courtesy, Colorado Bar Association

During the paranoid McCarthy era of the 1950s, seven supposed Communist conspirators were arrested in Denver under the direction of FBI Director J. Edgar Hoover and Denver Agent Charles Brown. Charged with conspiring to teach the violent overthrow of the United States government, the Colorado Seven were found guilty under the Smith Act. They are shown leaving the District Court on May 26, 1955, during their lengthy trial. From left to right are: Patricia Blau, Lewis M. Johnson, Arthur Bary, Anna Bary, Harold Zepelin, Maia Scherrer, and Joseph Scherrer. Courtesy, Colorado Historical Society

The concept is well put by U.S. District Judge John Kane: "Public service means at the very least that the public can rely upon the integrity of the legal profession even when it cannot rely upon the integrity of individuals connected with a particular transaction. It means adhering to and enforcing the moral and social values espoused by the public."

The words "pro bono" have come to mean helping the poor with legal services they can't afford, because we are taught in this democracy that everyone should have access to justice.

Using all senses of the words and concepts, the legal community in Denver has, for the most part, been active in trying to improve the profession, improve the judiciary, streamline laws, and deliver services to the poor.

Three examples of public service follow: Lawyers defending the unpopular "Communists" in a 1950s trial; the huge effort in the 1960s to change the way judges are selected; and the formation of the Thursday Night Bar in 1966.

Communists on Trial

The creeping terror of Communism was in full flower during the early 1950s, fueled by the ravings of Senator Joseph McCarthy. With hindsight, one can be glib about a nation running scared from the menace called "Reds" and "Commies," but the fear was real to those who read about it daily, had schoolchildren practicing drop drills to hide from bombs, and heard hyped-up FBI reports about widespread Communist infiltration in this country.

In this atmosphere, seven people were arrested in August 1954 "in the shadows of the Colorado State Capitol" by the FBI and charged with conspiring to teach the violent overthrow of the United States. Patricia Blau, Joseph and Maia Scherrer, Arthur and Anna Bary, Lewis Johnson, and Harold Zepelin were indicted under the Smith Act.

The defendants couldn't find lawyers. Judge Jean S. Breitenstein turned to the Denver Bar Association to find appropriate counsel. Denver Bar Association President Louis Issacson went to the large firms in town, which at that time had no more than 15 lawyers, and asked each to contribute a lawyer on a pro bono basis.

Those selected to defend the "Colorado Seven" were: William V. Hodges, elder statesman of the defense, William Alan Bryans III, John L. Ferguson, Robert H. Harry, Robert E. More, William B. Naugle, Forrest C. O'Dell, Luis D. Rovira, John Shafroth, Arthur K. Underwood, Jr., and Jay W. Tracey, Jr. Mary Kaufman, a New York attorney, was personally retained by Anna Bary. Hodges, Bryans and More were senior partners in their firms; the rest were mid-level to very junior attorneys.

Denver newspapers trumpeted the arrest, the charges, and the rumors, putting a spotlight on all that happened. Two-inch-high,

Jean S. Breitenstein (back row, center) began his career prosecuting bootleggers as an assistant U.S. attorney. He then spent 21 years in private practice before being named to the District Court, where he earned his reputation as "the judge's judge." Breitenstein served as the presiding judge in the 1955 case of the Colorado Seven. Courtesy, Denver Public Library, Western History Department

blood-red headlines screamed in October 1954: "Denver Reds Get 11 Top Attorneys."

From October to March, when the trial started, the 11 attorneys worked full-time on the case, reading Communist tracts and selections from Marx, Lenin, and Engels. The government had a long list of witnesses.

At the beginning of the two-month trial, called by the *Rocky Mountain News* "one of the greatest trial dramas ever held in Colorado," Hodges explained the foundation of the case: "[This trial] is primarily a constitutional case, on the solution of which will depend the determination of the line beyond which Congress cannot go in limiting free

Eleven lawyers, including some of Denver's most prominent attorneys, were appointed by Denver's District Court to defend the Colorado Seven in 1955. Although the defendants were ultimately found guilty, their counsel worked admirably for several months without compensation in the midst of an extremely volatile political situation. Standing, left to right - Luis D. Rovira, Robert H. Harry, Forrest C. O'Dell, John Shafroth, Jay W. Tracey, William B. Naugle, John L. Ferguson. Seated, left to right - William A. Bryans, III, Robert E. More, William V. Hodges, Arthur K. Underwood. Courtesy, Denver Bar Association

speech and assembly."

All defendants pleaded not guilty.

After much drama in front of the stern Judge Breitenstein (including one incident where an FBI witness identified Luis Rovira as one of the Communists, bringing the one smile from the judge during two months), the jury was out for 12 hours and returned with its verdict.

Headlines in late May 1955 read: "7 Denver Reds Found Guilty."

The defense lawyers were paid by their own firms, but the firms were not compensated by the federal courts, a situation deplored by Judge Breitenstein. The *Rocky Mountain News* echoed his concern:

[The] trial has been one of which the whole free world can be proud. It is one of which Colorado certainly is proud . . . And it is entirely right that the most prominent lawyers in the state—lawyers whose combined services would be beyond the economic reach of all but the very wealthiest—stand guard over the legal rights of these defendants . . . Fortunately, in this case, the Bar Association and the court were able to select 11 prominent law firms and could ask each to spare a member for the arduous task . . . They are among the most prominent men at the bar. They range in age from 30 to 70. And they bring to their task years of background and legal experience. It would fall to few private individuals to have such legal talent at the defense table. The least we can do is let them know that we appreciate their service. And that we take steps now to see that some compensation is provided for other cases of this kind so that the whole burden will not fall again exclusively on those who are fortunate enough to be able to afford to do their duty.

Why was the final verdict "guilty"?

Reporter Charlie Roos, who covered the trial for the *Denver Post,* recently explained: "It was Cold War time. Even the word Communist was kind of scary to many people. My perception now is that in a technical way, the government proved its case, but its case was lousy . . . Of course, part of this is looking retrospectively, but these people were nobodies who accomplished nothing. They were so ineffective. I feel the whole thing was conceived in hysteria and tried in an unhealthy climate."

The man who is chief justice of the Colorado Supreme Court now, Luis Rovira, was one of the rookie lawyers on the panel then. He was only four years out of law school and the case left a lasting impression on him:

"It was at the height of the McCarthy Era—the Communist conspiracy, the Communist scare, the black listing of screen writers. The Denver Bar was willing to stand up and defend the rights of these persons. It demonstrated the strength of our judicial system where lawyers and their firms were willing to commit this kind of time to this pro bono effort."

Rovira remembers that the *Rocky Mountain News* was "telling people how wonderful we were but then we'd go to cocktail parties and people would ask how we could defend those Commies."

All defendants appealed, and the conviction was overturned two years later. Rovira said the seven were tried a second time, with court-appointed counsel. They were found guilty. When they appealed, the decision was reversed again. "The U.S. Attorney didn't press for a third trial and the case was dismissed," Rovira said.

The Missouri Plan

Was he a good judge or just good at shaking hands, serving up spaghetti, and kissing babies?

Edward E. Pringle, for many years chief justice of the Colorado Supreme Court, said he felt depressed instead of jubilant when he was reelected to the Supreme Court in the early 1960s. He had spent months campaigning to secure his position. At that time, a judge would spend nights talking to the guys in firehouses and police stations, buying drinks in bars for political workers, and putting himself in political debt to people who would later need favors.

Even if anyone had asked about legal issues before the court he couldn't have answered because it was unethical. But they didn't ask.

Since the 1950s, members of the bar association had wanted to take judges out of the political arena. They had many objections to the present system.

Attorney Noah Atler sat on the Citizen's Committee for Non-Political Selection and Removal of Judges in 1966. He continued to practice law well into his eighties. Courtesy, Colorado Bar Association

First, the cost and expenditure of energy to run for office was daunting. Many quiet, scholarly, serious men and women—the type most would want for thoughtful jurists—probably never sought a judgeship because of the publicity. Some could have been deterred by the thought that, regardless of their performance, their career as judge could come to an abrupt end after one term.

Second, what would the campaign issues be for a judge? The election became a popularity contest with name recognition, rather than performance, as the key. The ability to campaign took precedence over the ability to judge.

A third objection was the idea that judges shouldn't be responsive to the "popular will." Judges are supposed to be responsive to the evidence and the legal arguments in their courtrooms, not to the views of people outside the court who haven't heard the case. One of the most cherished rights of Americans is the right to be tried in a courtroom atmosphere free of popular pressures, by a judge who hasn't made commitments to voters, who doesn't have to consult or express the popular will, and who acts fairly and impartially on the facts. Judges are supposed to act on the facts and the law and render fair decisions rather than popular ones.

Some bar members became very interested in a selection process Missouri had been using since 1940 called the "merit selection plan" (or the "Missouri Plan"), where judges would initially be appointed by the governor from a few names submitted by a committee which included laymen. Later, in regular elections, voters would choose to retain or not retain the judge.

Finally, in 1966, the Colorado Bar Association, the Denver Bar Association, and many Denver lawyers formed a committee called the "Citizen's Committee for Non-Political Selection and Removal of Judges." This committee, which included Noah Atler, Denver Bar Association President Norma Comstock, and M.B. Holt, among many others, got "Amendment 3" on the November ballot.

At the Denver Bar Association annual meeting, President Comstock, before passing the giant presidential gavel to Stewart Shaefer, made a special plea to the membership to get additional signatures on the amendment petition. At a later meeting, she said the citizen's committee was "running scared, if slightly optimistic." Some larger offices and banks had been supplying people full-time to circulate petitions. The Colorado Bar Association had advanced about $30,000, individual lawyers and firms had given about $27,000, and others about $7,000. They figured to spend about $50,000 more to cover radio, TV, newspapers, public relations, and office overhead. The DBA board took a look at its financial condition and decided to advance the committee $10,000.

The minutes reflect that the board of the Denver Bar Association decided not to have a judicial poll that year "because of the possible adverse effect it might have on the judicial amendment No. 3 campaign."

When the hoped-for passage of HB 8188 allowing income tax deduction of contributions to judicial reform campaigns failed, money for the campaign became harder to get. The committee returned again to the CBA and DBA boards and the boards again decided to underwrite the campaign. This would be the bar's investment in a once-in-a-decade chance to get non-partisan judicial selection into the constitution, the board decided, and it shouldn't be lost because they didn't make the last month's push to the voters.

The amendment to Article 6 of the Colorado Constitution did pass.

The merit selection of judges, now in place for 25 years, was routinely attacked in the Colorado legislature for years, but to date has had many more supporters than detractors. More than 30 states use this system and once begun, none has gone back to electing judges on a partisan basis.

Under this system judges are still accountable:

• to the voters, who decide regularly whether they will remain in office;
• to the lawyers, who practice before them, evaluate their performance, and make their evaluations public;
• to the Judicial Qualifications Commission, which can bring about their removal from the bench;
• to the higher courts, which can overturn their decisions.

From the vantage point of 1991, the system seems entrenched and no serious foreseeable efforts are being mounted in opposition.

Thursday Night Bar: Helping the Poor

Colorado was supplying counsel to indigent persons accused in non-capital felony cases even before the 1963 U.S. Supreme Court decision *Gideon v. Wainwright*, which required it. This was apparently true in most Western states.

Because judges had to campaign for election in those days, a "spoils" system had developed. Lawyers would donate money to a judge's campaign fund, and often that lawyer later would be appointed as counsel to defend an indigent person and be paid by the county for that defense.

This actually worked fairly well, according to U.S. District Court Judge John Kane.

Several things happened to change it, though. A case in Durango, where a man was charged with a particularly vicious murder, actually went to trial. Usually, the defendant pled guilty and a deal was made for sentencing, Kane said. But this time, the trial totally drained the county's budget for defense counsel for the whole year, pointing up an obvious economic problem in the system. In 1964, the U.S. Supreme Court decided *Escobedo v. State of Illinois,* which held that an accused person has the right to counsel at the time his liberty is restrained. Soon, various programs were being tried all over the country to fulfill the requirement. One program in Boulder was headed by Jim Carrigan, former Colorado Supreme Court justice and now U.S. District Court judge. Adams County, with a progressive board of county commissioners, set up a public defender system to cover the critical time when a person was brought into jail. They decided to work on felony cases as well as mental health cases, juvenile cases, and others. John Kane was selected as the part-time attorney to run the program. "It's the only 60-hour-a-week part-time job I've ever had," Kane said.

When this program had been in effect about a year, Judge Kane said, Denver started looking into it—because of the *Escobedo* decision, but also because of the *Miranda v. Arizona* decision, which was issued about that time, holding that a person had to be *advised* of the right to legal counsel. Also about this time, Colorado passed the judicial reform amendment so that judges no longer had the need to use a "spoils system" to make appointments. It would be more of a burden for them now, so they backed the public defender system.

Denver passed a city ordinance creating a Public Defender office. Ed Sherman, who had been active as an ACLU lawyer and was "a criminal lawyer of extraordinary skill" according to Judge Kane, was selected as Denver's first public defender. One of the first people he hired was Joseph Quinn, later chief justice of the Colorado Supreme Court. "That office has a very distinguished alumni group," Kane added.

On the civil side, the Legal Aid Society has been engaged in limited legal work since it was formally founded in 1925 by members of the Denver Bar. It has helped people with divorce, adoption, and other matters, with most referrals coming from the Department of Social

Services. It depends, to a large extent, on contributions from community agencies and volunteers. With money channeled during President Johnson's "War on Poverty," the Legal Aid Society was able to expand. The more Legal Aid did, the more everyone realized how great the need was for help with these matters. They went to the Denver Bar Association for help.

In 1966, Denver Bar Association President Norma Comstock returned from an American Bar Association meeting and talked to the Board of Trustees about the national attention being given to legal services to the poor. She said her priority as DBA president would be an attempt to expand legal services for the poor "under the so-called war

In 1965 Norma Comstock became the first woman president of the Denver Bar Association. Comstock, who specialized in probate and bankruptcy cases, said that she experienced little prejudice in her dealings with other attorneys, although clients were occasionally biased. Courtesy, Royal Rubright

on poverty program of the federal government."

A Young Lawyers committee led by Garth Grissom, which also involved Richard Young and Dale Tooley, studied the matter, and recommended a plan that Grissom remembers as ". . . just a daydream. We didn't know whether it could be implemented." Grissom said they were especially adamant about the idea that large numbers of members of the bar association should become involved. Figuring out how to implement the plan was then turned over to a group led by Don Giacomini, the "Special Committee on Professional Services to the Poor."

Giacomini went to the Denver Bar Association board on March

Ed Kahn, the 1984-1985 Denver Bar Association president, turns over the gavel to the 1985-1986 president Garth Grissom. Nearly 20 years earlier Grissom had led a Young Lawyers committee to develop a plan for legal services for the poor. Courtesy, Colorado Bar Association

17, 1966, with a proposal. He asked for $1,000. The board, of course, gave his committee $750. The proposal said, basically, "let's get started with a program of helping the poor and we'll iron out the wrinkles later." The board approved the committee's plan.

The official start-up date was May 26, 1966. Legal clinics, sponsored by the Young Lawyers Section, were held on Thursday evenings, from 7 to 9 p.m. at locations in both west and east Denver. The volunteer lawyers would handle about 18 cases each night, settling some on the spot, referring out to other lawyers matters that were more complicated and time consuming.

Many lawyers helped with the project, as did Helen Peterson, director of Denver's Commission on Community Relations, and her staff. Howard Rosenberg, then head of the Denver Legal Aid Society, loaned experience and the society's services.

From this storefront project begun 25 years ago, what came to be called the "Thursday Night Bar" is now an integral part of the Denver legal scene respected by the community and strongly supported by the bar with financial resources, staff, and almost 1,000 volunteer lawyers.

At its permanent home at 19th and Sherman, one block from the DBA offices, TNB has 900 attorneys and 20 law firms on its pro bono and reduced fee panels. Besides this volunteer help, they've also involved legal secretaries, paralegals, legal investigators, and court reporters—all of whom donate their time to the program.

In 1990 TNB referred 1,647 cases to volunteer attorneys. Almost one-third were bankruptcy, a sign of the economic times in Denver, 23 percent were domestic relations, and the rest were legal problems related to probate, real estate, housing, consumer law, wills, insurance, and tort defense.

People come to TNB from all over the metro area. In addition to the Denver Bar Association, which allocates one-quarter of its annual budget to the TNB, the surrounding county bar associations contribute both volunteer time and money.

In the interest of efficiency, a number of years ago TNB was moved to the Legal Aid Society offices where Legal Aid staff and TNB volunteers screen clients. TNB now has four full-time staff members. Director Gina Weitzenkorn explained the difference between the two agencies: the Legal Aid office is like a "legal emergency room," and TNB is aimed more at "chronic care."

The Legal Aid office grew in the 1960s and 1970s with city and federal money, then shrank with reduced federal aid and changed political winds in the early 1980s. But with strong defense by the bar association, it has become an essential component in efforts to insure equal justice for all.

Denver Bar Association members staff a booth at the Capitol Hill People's Fair. Proceeds were slated for three worthy causes: Child Abuse Prevention Volunteers, Points for People, and the Colorado Domestic Violence Coalition. Courtesy, Colorado Bar Association

Some of the ongoing projects held at the TNB offices and at the YWCA, sponsored by the DBA Public Interest Law Committee, include monthly clinics in which low-income clients are helped through the divorce process, or taught about small claims court, collections, or bankruptcy procedures. Family Law Court Week, a program to assist people with divorce and custody problems, is held throughout the year in the Denver District Court. Recently, panels of volunteer lawyers have been established to help provide legal assistance to AIDS victims and people with immigration problems.

These are only three examples of public service to the community by members of the Denver Bar Association. Literally thousands of large and small contributions by members of the bar could be described.

Most lawyers will tell you: "I've been given so much. I want to give something back." And they do. They tutor underprivileged children, coach organized sports, and volunteer on charitable and educational boards and groups that help the community and the environment. They organize drives for clothing and food, work on day care for the homeless, and staff a Saturday clinic where the homeless can come for legal advice. Members of the bar spend countless hours in schools, teaching students about the legal system, and many more hours at the bar association working on various ways to improve the legal system.

Pro bono publico is not a just an ancient and historic Latin phrase in Denver. It remains a call to action for members of the Denver Bar Association.

OPENING THE DOORS

L ittle stories, jokes, and casual references, scattered through the dusty and yellowing Denver Bar Association history books, tell the real story.

When African-Americans were mentioned it was almost always in the form of a joke. The African-American person was often called "Rastus." He called the other (white) person "boss," and it was all written in dialogue.

Women were helpless little darlings, conniving wives, or domineering mothers. Or they were the people who danced at the annual gatherings. First woman Denver Bar Association president Norma Comstock once had to announce the annual stag dinner at a board meeting. And for women attorneys, going to meetings at the all-male University Club meant going in through the steamy kitchen.

The early history of the bar association accurately reflects the attitude of society toward women and minorities at that time.

But there are some points of pride.

• Mary Lathrop was admitted to the bar association soon after the turn of the century, even if the men thought her odd and treated her that way.
• Several important men in the bar battled the hatred and political grip of the Ku Klux Klan in the 1930s.
• Ralph Carr, governor of Colorado and an attorney, alone among politicians, spoke out on behalf of persecuted Americans of Japanese origin during World War II.
• James Flanigan became the first African-American judge in Colorado in the 1950s.

The truth is that white men started the bar association and dominated it for most of its 100-year history. Women and minorities made incursions here and there but the real changes in bar membership have happened in the last decade.

Today, the doors of the bar association are wide open. Women make up approximately 20 percent of the membership, reflecting

Members of the Sam Cary Bar Association posed for this group portrait during their annual meeting in 1990. Left to right: J. Wallace Wortham, Hubert A. Farbes, Jr., Earle F. Jones, Linda Wade Hurd, W. Harold Flowers, Jr., Raymond D. Jones, Gary M. Jackson, and Wiley Y. Daniel. Courtesy, Colorado Bar Association

The University Club, which moved in 1895 to 17th Street and Sherman, limited its membership to males with university degrees. Because of this policy the women lawyers of the Denver Bar had to enter through the back entrance when the association held its 1931 annual meeting at the club. It was an affront that caused the abandonment of the club as a future site for association gatherings, spurred by the indignity suffered by Mary Lathrop and the other women bar members. Since that time, the University Club has changed its policy and now welcomes women members. Courtesy, Colorado Historical Society

their numbers in the profession. The Denver Bar Association includes Hispanics, African-Americans, Asian-Americans, Native Americans, and even those who aren't attorneys but are important to the legal profession-legal assistants, paralegals, and office managers.

In the past five years, the Denver Bar Association has had two women presidents as well as one African-American and one Hispanic president.

Minority Bar Associations

In response to a feeling that their voices were not being heard in the mainstream bar, "minority" bar associations were formed. Many minority attorneys belong to the Denver Bar Association and a minority bar association.

Dan Vigil, associate dean at the University of Colorado Law School and past president of the Hispanic Bar Association, explains why: "We exist as mutual support groups, to advance the interests of members of the group, such as full participation in the legal profession. We want to see more judges, more partners in major law firms, more law professors and more law students."

Sam Cary Bar Association

The Sam Cary Bar Association was founded in 1971 by seven African-American attorneys: Norman Early, Dan Muse, Raymond Jones, Gary Jackson, Phillip Jones, King Trimble, and Billy Lewis. At that time, fewer than 15 African-American attorneys were practicing in Colorado. The first meetings were held in members' homes and law offices.

Today, there are about 175 African-American lawyers in the state and they hold regular monthly meetings at the Denver and Colorado Bar

Association offices. They work with law school administrators to maintain and increase African-American enrollments. The SCBA awards a scholarship to deserving African-American law students at both the CU and DU law schools. They also sponsor a Continuing Legal Education retreat each year, a "homecoming" event that allows the state's African-American lawyers to network, and an annual minority orientation seminar to help students successfully complete law school and find employment.

The association is named for attorney Sam Cary, who was admitted to the Colorado Bar in for attorney Sam Cary, who was admitted to the Colorado Bar in 1919. The first African-American to be a Denver Bar Association member was James C. Flanigan, who later became the first African-American judge in Colorado. He joined the Denver Bar Association in 1947 and remembers attending meetings where he sat in the back of the room by himself because seats at the front were "taken." But he did not let that stop him from pursuing his dream of becoming a judge and he believes the DBA is what it is today because there are more "right thinking than wrong thinking people in our profession."

LEFT: *The 1980 convention of the Colorado Women's Bar Association took place at Loretto Heights College. Courtesy, Colorado Bar Association*

LEFT: *Judge Lynn Hufnagle (left) and attorney Barbara Salomon (right) confer at an early organizational meeting of the Colorado Women's Bar Association. Courtesy, Colorado Bar Association*

Colorado Hispanic Bar Association

The Hispanic Bar Association (first called the Chicano Bar Association) was incorporated in 1977.

Hispanics have unquestionably made progress, said Associate Dean Dan Vigil, "particularly over the past 10 years. But there are still only 15 or so Hispanic judges out of 270 judges in the state. There are only four Hispanic law professors in the state. There were none in 1986 and one in 1987. But there's little progress in terms of entry into the large firms. We have a long way to go."

Hispanic lawyers now number about 300 in Colorado, he said. In the fall 1991 class at the University of Colorado, 20 of the more than 150 first-year students will be Hispanic. At the University of Denver, Assistant Dean Rufina Hernandez reported that 50 minority students were enrolled in the first-year class.

The first Hispanic member of the Denver Bar Association was Charles Vigil, who graduated from the University of Colorado Law

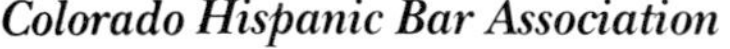

FACING PAGE: *Against the wishes of Governor Ralph Carr, thousands of evacuated Japanese-Americans from throughout the West were confined in the Amachi Relocation Camp near Granada, Colorado. Carr firmly believed in the constitutional rights of Japanese-Americans and felt they should not be judged according to their ancestry. As a tribute to his humanitarian ideals, a plaque thanking Carr for his efforts was placed outside of the governor's office in the State Capitol. In addition, a statue honoring Carr was erected by Japanese-Americans in 1974 in Sakura Square. Courtesy, Denver Public Library, Western History Department*

School in 1935 and has practiced in Denver and Trinidad ever since. He was also the first Hispanic to be appointed a U.S. attorney.

Colorado Women's Bar Association

The Colorado Women's Bar Association was started in 1978. One organizer remembers the evening as chilly outside, but the women shared wine and ideas and it was anything but cold inside. One reason they gathered was the perceived discrimination of a number of male judges toward the female attorneys who appeared before them. The women were feeling more discrimination than in the past, the organizer said, probably because of increasing numbers of women in the profession. That year, 500 women were registered to practice in Colorado.

Women who attended that first meeting included Shayne Madsen, Barbara Salomon, Karen Mathis, Judy Schulman, Barbara Jacobi, Francis Koncilja, Pam Gordon, Jo Ann Weinstein, Kathy Bonham, Sandy Rothenberg, Ruth Beuchler, Susan Cardinal, Amy Greenfield, Beth McCann, Gay Ummel, Madeline Caughey, Carol Gersti, and prime organizer Natalie Ellwood.

Today, 4,259 women attorneys are registered to practice law in Colorado. Women comprise 23 percent of the lawyers in the state, and women make up about one-half of the law school population in Colorado.

About 600 women and men belong to the CWBA and work on committees that devote time to the professional and personal advancement of women attorneys, helping indigent women in the state and promoting high standards in the legal system. The CWBA holds an annual convention, publishes a monthly newsletter, lobbies for various legislation, and addresses political issues. The association works especially hard to promote women for the judiciary.

One early member of CWBA said that it remains a place where women can let down their hair and "speak their truth." They can't always say it to men "because it makes men uncomfortable and most women aren't into making men uncomfortable."

Mary Lathrop, called "that damn woman" when she started, was the first woman to join the Denver Bar Association and one of the first two women to join the American Bar Association in 1918. She had been asked to join in 1901, but declined. Treated as an oddity at first, she became a stalwart in the bar, was the official hostess when

Attorney Jane Michaels of Holland & Hart served as president of the Denver Bar Association during its centennial year.

In 1947 Mary Lathrop was presented with a meritorious service award for her work with the U.S.O. during World War II. She organized and cooked five-course meals for servicemen and was able to provide her guests with free legal advice. Christmas and Thanksgiving dinners sometimes attracted as many as 100 soldiers, who would show up at her home to experience her warmth and hospitality. Courtesy, Denver Public Library, Western History Department

the American Bar Association met in Denver in 1926, and practiced law for 55 years. Norma Comstock was the DBA's first woman president in 1965—there wouldn't be another for 24 years.

All minority bar associations, including the newly formed Asian-American, Black Women, and Native American bar associations, have seats on the Colorado Bar Association Board of Governors. Leaders in the Denver and Colorado bar associations work actively to increase minority participation in the "majority" bar associations.

PLAINTIFF

THE 1991 LAWYER

What's going on here?

College graduates who want to be lawyers are pounding on the doors of the University of Colorado and the University of Denver law schools. Three thousand of them applied for the 150 available places at the University of Colorado for the fall 1991 semester. At the University of Denver, some 2,600 went after 300 seats.

Law school applicants may be driven by the glamour and power depicted at every flip of the TV channel. Perhaps they see themselves at big firms, arguing persuasively before crowded courtrooms, driving BMWs to their mountain homes.

The real picture of a lawyer's life in Denver has considerably less flash and will probably include more competition than in the past.

Some would say the field in Denver is crowded—there are about 7,000 lawyers in a metropolitan area with a population of 1.8 million. About one-third of the attorneys in Colorado work solo. Another 29 percent are in firms with two to five lawyers. Only 10 percent are in the large (over 50 attorneys) firms.

Compared to the oil boom days in the late 1970s and early 1980s, the atmosphere in Denver is a bit cooler for lawyers. Openings in law firms come less frequently. Scaling down is occurring these days.

Today's typical graduate will do some moving from firm to firm, to increase opportunities for compensation and job satisfaction.

He/she (half of those in law school are women) will certainly work with computers and word processors, know how to use a FAX machine, probably have a car phone, work with paralegals and legal assistants, and learn how to research cases using WESTLAW or LEXIS.

"Law office management" is a fairly new concept for some attorneys. Instituting more efficient office practices comes in response to economic pressure and new technology; it's also a result of the growing threat of malpractice suits.

An old problem that nags many lawyers is the image of the profession. Since the first lawyer spoke for the first client, lawyers have

Participants in a recent mock trial competition experienced some intense moments. Courtesy, Colorado Bar Association

ABOVE: Lawyers who have just passed the bar are treated to "Breakfast at the Bar." Courtesy, Colorado Bar Association

FACING PAGE: The challenging practice of law in Denver has come far from the days of the raucous vigilance committees and the rudimentary Miners' Courts of the mid-1800s. Glass-adorned office towers now house many of the city's law offices. Photo by Steve Zavodny

RIGHT: New lawyers attend an orientation session conducted by the Denver Bar Association Young Lawyer's Division and Chief Judge John N. McMullen of the Denver District Court.

worried about how they're seen by others. Besides the fact that lawyers rate down near newspaper reporters and used-car salesmen in "who do you trust" polls, the knife has been twisted deeper by the recent spate of lawyer jokes.

Never mind, for the moment, this attack from without. Probably the changes coming from within are more important.

At a recent Denver Bar Association Board of Trustees meeting, members were asked where they thought the profession would be in 5 or 10 years. The tone was rather somber. Some despaired at the technology that encouraged everything to go so quickly. A few felt that women would either leave the profession or they would change it from within—in reaction to what they see as the pressure, workload, and dehumanizing aspects of being an attorney. The catch-phrase "professionalism" is being used at bar meetings nationwide and covers a general malaise.

Still, as one 10-year attorney pointed out, "I'm a lawyer because it's fun. It's fun to win. I knew there would be some routine and grind, as there is in any job. But I enjoy this more than anything I've ever done."

ABOVE: *Held in the shadow of Colorado's legal system in Civic Center Park, the annual People's Fair is a popular Denver celebration. Photo by Mark E. Gibson*

RIGHT: *Many of the city's historic homes now house today's law offices. The Denver firm of Long & Jaudon at 1600 Ogden is just one fine example of this historic preservation. Photo by Steve Zavodny*

LEFT: The Colorado Judicial Building in Denver is an outstanding achievement of modern architecture. Photo by Tom Stack/Tom Stack & Associates

BELOW: The Tabor Center replaced Denver's first skyscraper, which was built in the 1800s. The Tabor Block, built for Horace Tabor by architect Willoughby J. Edbrooke, was constructed at a time when the first fledgling bar associations struggled for acceptance in Denver. The building marked the commercial growth of downtown Denver just as the Tabor Center marks Denver's redevelopment a century later. Photo by Tom E. Myers/Tom Stack & Associates

ABOVE: Dedicated on June 24, 1911, the Pioneer Monument at Colfax and Broadway has stood as a tribute to the city's early settlers. The Native American figure that was originally designed to top Frederick MacMonnies' bronze sculpture offended early Denverites, so it was replaced by this likeness of Kit Carson on horseback. Photo by Tom E. Myers/Tom Stack & Associates

RIGHT: Originally considered a boondoggle of Mayor Benjamin F. Stapleton's term of office, the City and County Building was constructed with a $2.5-million bond. It was dedicated on August 1, 1932. As Mayor Begole replaced Stapleton and first occupied the new building, Denver and the nation entered the Great Depression. Photo by Mark E. Gibson

FACING PAGE: A favorite lunchtime retreat for the city's legal community, historic Larimer Square stands on what was once the original townsite of Denver. Photo by Steve Zavodny

DOS EQUIS
XX
DOS EQUIS
DOS EQUIS
XX
IMPORTED BEER
DOS EQUIS

The monolithic office towers of Broadway soar into the blue Denver sky. Photo by Steve Zavodny

Denver's early lawyers would be proud of the city they helped to establish years ago when the West was still wild and pioneer justice was swift and sure. Photo by Steve Zavodny

Since Denver is now so large, there really isn't a cohesive, definable "legal community" anymore—and that's where the organized bar comes in. Many lawyers find satisfaction in participating in DBA activities.

Two recently-formed committees that have generated excitement are the Seniors and the Committee for the Environment.

The Seniors recently drew about 80 members over 65 to a "roast" of Tony Zarlengo at the University Club. "Finally, I could walk in a room and know everyone there!," one senior remarked. They drank and dined and recounted stories that have almost become legends.

On the other hand, the Committee for the Environment is dominated by younger members and has as its goal leading Denver lawyers into the land of recycling. Figuring lawyers are second only to government workers in using (and wasting) paper, this dynamic group has convinced the courts to encourage briefs (double-sided) on recycled paper and is trying to educate its members and other Denver lawyers.

Four activities started in recent years give a flavor of the modern bar:

Twice a year Denver's historic Paramount Theater becomes the site of the swearing in of Colorado's new lawyers. Courtesy, Colorado Bar Association

• Teen Court. Begun and guided by the Community Concerns Committee, Teen Court is an alternative to school disciplinary procedures. Teens can be "tried" in this twice-monthly court that uses teen prosecutors and defense attorneys, a peer jury, and a real judge. Lawyer volunteers help each side with its case. The first session was featured on NBC's Today Show. Police and school officials are enthusiastic about the program and have urged the bar to expand it city-wide.

• Barristers' Benefit Ball. This fancy party, usually held on Saturday night during Law Week, is an effort to bring Denver lawyers together. In its

A driving force in Denver's legal community, former University of Denver School of Law professor Thompson Marsh played a pivotal role in the establishment of the first title standards by a bar association in the 1940s. Courtesy, Thompson Marsh

FAR RIGHT: Dean of the University of Denver School of Law, Dennis Lynch approves of recent changes in the practice of law. With the benefits of new technology and the availability of alternative dispute resolution, he feels more and more people are being better served by Denver's legal community. Photo by Steve Zavodny

third year (which featured a silent auction), the BBB raised more than $80,000, with the Thursday Night Bar as beneficiary.

• Sports Festival. Another effort to bring members together for some frivolity, the festival has been held in early summer the last four years. The Sports Committee oversees the event, which includes a golf tournament, various races, volleyball, softball, croquet, and other games. The day is mellow and relaxed, with some competition and much camaraderie.

• Centennial Celebration. To commemorate the Denver Bar Association's 100th year and to bring a sense of history to its members, the Centennial Committee took on many projects: this history book; a legacy to the city; a birthday party/town hall meeting in October; a video tribute to its first 100 years which honored first members of various minority groups; the sale of coffee mugs, shirts, and coasters with the new DBA logo; and an emphasis on the 100th anniversary at the Barristers' Ball and during Law Week.

The Denver Bar Association has some 6,000 members, about 12 staff members (plus six in the Continuing Legal Education arm), and is housed at 1900 Grant Street on the ninth floor. Because of Denver's fairly "flat" real estate market, and because the bar associations seem to be growing each year, a committee is looking into buying an office building for both the Denver and Colorado bar associations.

What's the biggest challenge for Denver lawyers?

According to Chuck Turner, executive director of the Denver and Colorado bar associations for the past 11 years, it is the changes

Denver's lawyers turn out to "Run for Legal Aid" every June. One thousand runners participated in the 1991 event. Courtesy, Colorado Bar Association

facing lawyers today in a high-tech, fast-paced world. The challenge for the Denver Bar Association will be in guiding members through the changes and offering the right kind of information and support.

"For all the perceived changes, there is plenty of room for our members to take pride in righting a wrong, representing a person in trouble, or simply being a "lawyer," Turner said.

Phil Dufford, longtime member of the Denver Bar Association and former president of the Colorado Bar Association, gave a speech a few years back to new members of the bar in which he acknowledged the problems and the challenges of the legal profession.

He wanted the new lawyers to know that they would be improving a good system, not salvaging a bad one.

"I believe in this profession and would like to pass on to younger attorneys the respect and love I have for the law.

"I believe no other profession does as much to police itself as we do.

"I believe no other profession contributes as much public service to those who are less fortunate in our society than we do.

ABOVE: Chuck Turner, executive director of the Colorado and Denver Bar Associations since 1980.

FAR RIGHT: The Denver Law Club puts on a show at the Colorado Bar Association convention every other year. Courtesy, Colorado Bar Association

RIGHT: Each spring the Denver Bar Association holds its ever-popular Chili Cook-off, giving Denver's legal community the opportunity to show off their culinary talents. Courtesy, Colorado Bar Association

"I believe that no other profession dedicates as much time and energy to improving its discipline as we do.

"We chose law originally and continue to choose it because it is a good and noble calling," Dufford said. "It challenges our intelligence, appeals to our sense of justice and fair play and in the end satisfies our sense of public service."

Dufford invited the new lawyers to become active in the bar association, to "come to the front line and help us battle for the preservation and betterment of our legal and judicial system."

"I chose the law a few years back and I've never been sorry," Dufford added. "My hope for you all is that you will be as happy and fulfilled in this profession as I am."

In a sense, Dufford's comments epitomize the goals and spirit of the Denver Bar Association.

As it begins its second century, the Denver Bar Association can look back at a rich history, knowing that it has weathered many challenges and circumstances and emerged stronger for them, and build its hope for the future on that strength.

Here's to the second 100 years!

Denver's flourishing skyline rises to the challenge of the city's innovative and streamlined legal community, led by the driving force of today's Denver Bar Association. Photo by Paul H. Henning/Third Coast Stock Source

NOTICE!
LAWYERS
MUST NOT BE
LONGWINDED

THE JUDICIARY

As Denver began to develop, a series of People's Courts arose to deal with the city's growing criminal and legal problems. Although they were often held in informal locations such as this saloon, the courts' decisions were generally held in high esteem by the participants. Note the sign on the wall that states, "Notice! Lawyers Must Not Be Longwinded." Courtesy, Denver Public Library, Western History Department

Tenth Circuit Court of Appeals

The law during the first three decades of the nineteenth century consisted primarily of settlers claims associations (squatters courts) and people's courts. In some places in Kansas, jurisdiction was determined by how far smoke could be seen from the chimney of the meeting place.

Although there have been circuit courts since this country's beginning, the modern circuit did not come into existence until 1891. It was not until April 1, 1929, that the Tenth became a separate new circuit in the United States court system. The states in the Tenth Circuit were once part of the old Eighth Circuit, a geographic monolith bounded on the north by Canada and on the south by Mexico, on the east by the Mississippi River, and on the west by the eastern edge of Nevada. Today, the Tenth Circuit includes Wyoming, Utah, Colorado, Kansas, Oklahoma, and New Mexico.

The early history of the federal territorial courts was greatly shaped by the unique history of the particular states: Kansas was the center of a free state-slave controversy immediately preceding the Civil War; Colorado was influenced by the Gold Rush; Wyoming was the real cowboy west; in Utah the controversy between the federal government and the Mormon settlers amounted to a kind of war; Oklahoma's legal history was strongly affected by the boomers and sooners attempting to settle on, claim, or steal Indian land; and New Mexico had both Hispanic and Indian heritages and some military influence.

Robert Lewis of Colorado and John Cotteral of Oklahoma were already serving on the Eighth Circuit, and by act of Congress their appointments were transferred to the Tenth. Two new judges were appointed: Orie Phillips of New Mexico and George McDermott of Kansas. The expansion of the numbers of judges has approximately paralleled the expansion of

the activities of the federal courts, and the Eleventh and Twelfth circuit positions were added in 1990.

The Tenth Circuit has a wide jurisdiction over all federal cases with federal questions, diversity cases with more than $50,000 in controversy, and appeals from many federal agencies. (Agency cases didn't develop until the 1930s, and later, as government agencies were formed.)

The early court heard many of the same kinds of cases heard today, including bankruptcy, diversity of citizenship, and federal criminal matters. The first case actually filed in the Tenth Circuit involved income taxes allegedly owed by a Colorado Springs developer.

Dramatic change came to the circuit courts in 1954 when the Supreme Court's decision in *Brown v. Board of Education* immersed the court in school desegregation cases. That decision led to the court's supervision of remedies for other unconstitutional conditions existing in society. Today the court oversees prisons, mental institutions, and apportionment of legislatures.

The Civil Rights Act of 1964 and the Supreme Court's new interpretations of civil rights laws greatly

increased the circuit court's load of habeas corpus cases. Two decades later, the drug war significantly increased the court's criminal caseload. Allowing appeals of sentences in the federal courts is the latest development that has significantly affected the court's work.

The early Tenth Circuit hung its hat at the old Post Office and Federal Courthouse at 18th and Stout streets until 1965, when it moved to a new courthouse. The court will return to its old home at the historic Post Office courthouse as soon as it can be remodeled, probably in 1994.

Much of this information is taken from a speech given by the Honorable James K. Logan delivered at the Tenth Circuit Judicial Conference in Santa Fa, New Mexico, on September 7, 1989. Logan is judge for the U.S. Court of Appeals for the Tenth Circuit.

Members of the Tenth Circuit Court of Appeals pictured are, from left to right: front row, Monroe G. McKay, Chief Judge William J. Holloway, Jr., and James K. Logan; middle row, Deanell R. Tacha, Stephanie K. Seymour; back row, John P. Moore, Wade Brorby, Stephen H. Anderson, Bobby R. Baldock, and David M. Ebel. Photo by Steve Zavodny

Colorado Supreme Court

During the mid-1850s Denver was called "the place where no law of the great American union claims jurisdiction." While this was not entirely true, there was a tendency for people in the Colorado Territory to boast of their independence. Yet there were many people in Colorado who saw the need for establishing a judicial framework for the territory. It would seem that President Abraham Lincoln and the U.S. Congress recognized this need as well. Thus in 1861 Congress organized the Territorial Supreme Court of Colorado to handle appellate matters for this frontier territory.

That same year, President Lincoln appointed the first three justices to the Territorial Supreme Court. Presidential appointment of territorial judges did not always sit well with the people of Colorado. There was a great deal of fear that Eastern "carpetbagger" judges would corrupt the West with their political interests and would retain loyalties outside of the community. Although such consensus may have been unwarranted, in the minds of Coloradans it became one of many incentives for becoming a state.

Colorado finally achieved statehood in 1876. With the establishment of the new state constitution, the Colorado Supreme Court was organized. The Colorado constitution defined the structure and jurisdiction of all state courts and granted the Supreme Court supervisory power over lower courts in the state, but that power was not exercised until 1953.

The Colorado Supreme Court of 1876 closely resembled its territorial predecessor. For example, the new court retained the basic structure of the Territorial Court, with three judges presiding. The most noticeable difference between the two courts was that the post-statehood court had elected judges rather than judges appointed from Washington. The first three judges elected were Henry C. Thatcher, Samuel H. Elbert,

Members of the Colorado Supreme Court pictured are, from left to right: William H. Erickson, Howard M. Kirshbaum, Mary J. Mullarkey, Anthony F. Vollack, Chief Justice Luis D. Rovira, George E. Lohr, and Joseph R. Quinn. Photo by Steve Zavodny

and Ebeneezer T. Wells.

Before the turn of the century, the Colorado Supreme Court was a nomadic body, in that it moved from one temporary office to another. In 1900, the court moved into the newly completed state capitol building. It stayed in the capitol until 1977.

In 1905, the Colorado constitution was amended to increase the number of justices on the court from three to seven. This amendment came in response to the growing backlog of cases facing the court. With the court's expansion, the justices were able to sit in departments of three judges to hear most cases. This practice of sitting in three-judge panels was discontinued, however, and the court now hears all cases en banc.

The 1959 Judicial Department Reform Act, passed by the Colorado General Assembly, created an administrative office to assist the courts. In 1966, Colorado adopted a merit-based selection and retention system for judges, commonly known as the "Missouri Plan." Previously, judges ran for judicial offices in partisan elections.

Today, the Colorado Supreme Court is comprised of seven justices, nominated by a commission and appointed by the governor to serve 10-year terms. The court has both appellate and original jurisdiction. Whereas the scope of the court's appellate jurisdiction may be changed by legislation, its original jurisdiction is fixed by the Colorado constitution. The Colorado Supreme Court is the court of last resort and the final arbiter of conflicts arising under the Colorado constitution or statutes within the state.

In 1977, the Colorado Supreme Court moved into the newly constructed Colorado Judiciary Building, located adjacent to the capitol. The Supreme Court Library, which was founded in 1861, moved with it. The building is well known for the large mural located above the Supreme Court Library. Painted by Angelo diBenedetto and dedicated in 1978, the mural depicts 60 famous jurists, philosophers, and historical figures who made outstanding contributions in the evolution of justice around the world.

Information provided by the Colorado Judicial Department, Office of the Public Education Coordinator; Rebecca V. Smith and L. Mike Brooks, contributors.

U.S. District Court • U.S. Bankruptcy Court • U.S. Magistrate Judges

U.S. District Court for the District of Colorado

U.S. District Court for the District of Colorado was established in 1876 by an Act of Congress. Judge Elmer S. Dundy of the District of Nebraska presided over the first session on December 5, 1876.

Judge Moses Hallett was the first judge appointed to the court in 1877. Judge Hallett's decisions on questions of mining and water law became the cornerstone for much of the economic development of the entire western United States.

The court is part of the Tenth Judicial Circuit. It is currently served by seven active District Court judges, two Senior District judges, and three full-time U.S. magistrates.

Unlike many states that are divided into two or more districts, Colorado is a single district. The U.S. District Court for the District of Colorado is a court of limited jurisdiction that hears civil and criminal cases brought under federal law. Approximately 2,500 civil and 500 criminal cases are filed in the court each year. The court's Probation Department averages 1,000 probationers and parolees under its supervision at all times.

U.S. Bankruptcy Court

Three bankruptcy laws were enacted during the 1800s to help people recover from significantly difficult economic periods. One of these, the 1898 Bankruptcy Act, established jurisdiction for federal district courts to hear bankruptcy matters.

In 1978, Public Law 95-598, effective 1979, superseded the Bankruptcy Act and established Bankruptcy Court as its own, separate court. In 1984 the U.S. Supreme Court ruled that it was unconstitutional for the court to function as an independent entity. As a result, Congress in 1986 enacted legislation modifying the 1978 act, returning the Bankruptcy Court under the general umbrella of the U.S. District Court.

Members of the U.S. Bankruptcy Court pictured are, clockwise from far right: Sidney B. Brooks, Patricia Ann Clark, Chief Judge Charles E. Matheson, Donald E. Cordova, and Roland J. Brumbaugh. Photo by Steve Zavodny

Referees presided over bankruptcy matters until the 1970s, at which time their titles were changed to bankruptcy judges. Today the court is presided over by five judges and a staff of 115. Legislation creating a sixth judgeship is currently pending before Congress.

During the early years, the court handled more administrative matters than judicial resolutions. The modern U.S. Bankruptcy Court generally handles only contested issues. The court's jurisdiction includes all issues and controversies that arise in matters that pertain to a bankruptcy.

Colorado's bankruptcy court is the largest federal court in the state, and one of the 10 largest bankruptcy courts in the country. The court's workload has tripled since 1984, when approximately 6,000 cases appeared on the docket. The court presently hears more than 18,000 cases a year.

In 1991 the court moved into the U.S. Custom House at 721 19th Street.

U.S. Magistrate Judges

The office of the U.S. magistrate was established by the Federal Magistrates Act of 1968 and is built upon the foundation of the 175-year-old United States Commissioner system. Commissioners had been used in the federal courts to try petty offense cases committed on federal property, to issue search warrants and arrest warrants, to determine bail for federal defendants, and to conduct other initial proceedings in federal criminal cases.

The Federal Magistrates Act created a new federal judicial officer to assume the duties formerly exercised by the commissioners and to conduct a wide range of judicial proceedings to expedite the disposition of the civil and criminal caseloads of U.S. District Courts. The actual de-

Members of the U.S. District Court for the District of Colorado pictured are, from left to right: front row, Alfred A. Arraj, Hatfield Chilson; middle row, Jim R. Carrigan, Richard P. Matsch, Chief Judge Sherman G. Finesilver, and John L. Kane, Jr.; back row, Edward W. Nottingham, Zita L. Weinshienk, Lewis T. Babcock, and Daniel B. Sparr. Photo by Steve Zavodny

termination of which duties to assign to magistrate judges is left up to the individual courts.

Magistrate judges are appointed for a term of eight years by a majority vote of the active sitting U.S. District judges of the court. The number of magistrate judge positions is determined by the Judicial Conference of the United States. At present three full-time U.S. magistrate judges sit in Colorado. A fourth full-time position has been approved for Colorado Springs/Pueblo. Three part-time magistrate judges sit at Durango, Estes Park, and Grand Junction.

The jurisdiction by statute includes:
1. The conduct of preliminary proceedings in criminal cases (such as the issue of warrants, conducting initial appearances, appointing counsel, and setting bond).
2. The trial and disposition of misdemeanors upon consent of the parties.
3. All civil pretrial proceedings as referred by the district judges.
4. Trial and disposition of civil cases upon consent of the parties and U.S. District judge to whom the case is assigned (presently not authorized by local rules).

The first full-time U.S. magistrate judge was Judge Royce Sickler, who was appointed in 1968. Sickler retired in 1984. Judge Hilbert Schauer was appointed to a new judgeship in 1975, and retired in 1991. Judge Bruce Pringle was appointed to fill the vacancy in 1991. Judge Donald Abram was appointed to a new judgeship in 1981. Judge Richard Harvey served from 1984 to 1990; Judge Richard Borchers was appointed in 1990.

Members of the U.S. Magistrates pictured are, from left to right: Donald E. Abram, Hilbert Schauer, and Richard M. Borchers. Photo by Steve Zavodny

Colorado Court of Appeals

The first Colorado Court of Appeals was created in 1891 by the General Assembly for an undetermined term. The three-judge court was established to assist the Supreme Court in clearing up its backlog. When the backlog was cleared in 1904, the court was abolished.

The second Court of Appeals, consisting of five judges, was formed in 1911. This court was established for the same purpose as the first but for a specified period of four years.

In 1970 the General Assembly again authorized the formation of the Court of Appeals, this time consisting of six judges, to assist the Supreme Court in reducing its backlog of pending cases. The court's jurisdiction was limited to civil matters. In 1974, four more judges were added, and the court's jurisdiction was expanded to include criminal cases.

By 1987, the Court of Appeals was burdened by its own backlog. The General Assembly authorized an increase in the number of judges on the court from 10 to 16. Three judges were appointed by the governor and took office on January 1, 1988. Six months later, on July 1, 1988, three additional judges took office.

Today, 16 judges serve on the Colorado Court of Appeals, and each judge serves an eight-year term.

The chief judge, who is appointed by the chief justice of the Colorado Supreme Court, assigns the judges to five divisions and rotates assignments from time to time. The court sits in panels of three to hear cases that have been appealed from district courts, Denver Probate Court, Denver Juvenile Court, and 16 state agencies and boards.

The Court of Appeals is not a trial court; it has initial appellate jurisdiction, with exceptions, over appeals from the Colorado district courts and juvenile and probate courts of the city and county of Denver. In addition, the court has initial jurisdiction over appeals from certain final orders of specific state agencies and boards.

Appeals from the decision of the Court of Appeals are directed to the Colorado Supreme Court. Under certain circumstances, the Court of Appeals may request transfer of an appeal to the state Supreme Court for review before final determination. The state Supreme Court then determines which court should have jurisdiction.

The first appellate court's first official courthouse was located in the state capitol building. In 1977, the Colorado Court of Appeals moved into the Colorado Judiciary Building, across the street from the capitol.

Members of the Colorado Court of Appeals pictured are, from left to right: front row, Dale P. Tursi, Charles D. Pierce, Chief Judge Alan L. Sternberg, Donald P. Smith, and Karen S. Metzger; middle row, Raymond Dean Jones, Leonard P. Plank, John A. Criswell, Claus J. Hume, and Peter H. Ney; back row, Sandra I. Rothenberg, Edwin G. Ruland, Jose D. L. Marquez, Harold D. Reed, Janice B. Davidson, and Frank N. Dubofsky. Photo by Fred C. Larkin

Denver County Court

Denver County Court was not established until 1904 because Denver County itself did not exist until then. After it emancipated from vast Arapahoe County in 1904, the city and county of Denver established a municipal court which served the city for the first half of the 1900s. At that time, Denver County Court operated along the lines of a probate court alongside justices of the peace.

tion has changed.

Denver County Court was a front-runner in the merit selection process of selecting judges. In 1965, Mayor Thomas Currigan established the first judicial nominating commission in the state of Colorado. The order was subsequently institutionalized by charter amendment. As originally envisioned, Denver County Court judges would serve a two-year proba-

Bernett was appointed presiding judge. He served for nine years, until 1970, when Judge George Manerbino became presiding judge. In 1984, newly elected Mayor Federico Peña appointed Edward Simons to be presiding judge. When Judge Simons was appointed to the Denver District Court in 1990, Judge Brian Campbell was selected as the new presiding judge.

In 1955 the justices of the peace were consolidated with the municipal court judges. The consolidation was a precursor to a similar statewide merger that took place in the early 1960s, which established the present county court system. Since then, jurisdiction has increased from $500 maximum to $10,000 maximum. Because Denver County Court is a court of limited jurisdiction, its complexion has changed as its jurisdic-

tionary period followed by a four-year term. The system differed from the present-day formula, however, in that the general population of Denver did not vote on whether or not to retain judges.

Judge Gerald McAuliff was the first presiding judge of the present-day Denver County Court, although he actually began as one of the previously mentioned municipal court judges. In 1961 Judge Charles

Members of the Denver County Court pictured are, from left to right: front row, Celeste C de Baca, Patricia Madsen, Presiding Judge Brian T. Campbell, Aleene Ortiz-White, Alfred Harrell, James Breese, Arthur Fine, Robert Patterson, and Raymond Satter; back row, Andrew Armatas, Larry Bohning, Irving Ettenberg, Jacqueline St. Joan, Robert B. Crew, Jr., Kathleen Bowers, John Marcucci, and Doris Burd. Courtesy, Gerald N. Mellman, Esq.

Denver District Court • Denver Juvenile Court • Denver Probate Court

Denver District Court

Denver District Court was established in 1879, three years after Colorado achieved statehood. At the time the courthouse was completed in 1883, the City of Denver was still part of Arapahoe County.

Denver District Court, a court of general jurisdiction, handles civil, domestic, and criminal cases for the district of Denver, one of 22 districts in Colorado. The court does not handle probate, juvenile, or mental health cases, which makes it unique in the state.

The court has a long history as a groundbreaker among the judiciary. The first black judge (Hon. James C. Flanigan) and the first woman judge (Hon. Zita L. Weinshienk) in the state first sat in Denver District Court. Judge Weinshienk is now a U.S. District Court Judge, the first woman to hold the office in Colorado.

The number of judges on the court has increased significantly since the court was established. In 1879, one judge presided over the entire district. Today, more than 20 Denver District Court judges sit on the bench.

Denver Juvenile Court

Denver is the only judicial district in Colorado that has its own separate Juvenile Court. Juvenile Court was established in 1902 by Judge Ben Lindsey, a municipal court judge who was concerned about children wandering the streets and other child welfare matters. He convinced the state legislature to pass an amendment establishing a Juvenile Court, the second of its kind in the United States.

The first Juvenile Court courthouse was located at 15th and Larimer streets. In 1932, it moved to the City and County Building, where it remains today.

Juvenile Court has original and exclusive jurisdiction on crimes and cases committed by juveniles aged 10 to 18. Areas of jurisdiction include dependency and neglect, paternity and support, and relinquishment and adoption.

The Gault Decision, handed down

Members of the Denver Juvenile Court pictured are, from left to right: Dana U. Wakefield, Presiding Judge Orrelle R. Weeks, and David E. Ramirez. Photo by Steve Zavodny

by the U.S. Supreme Court, was the single most significant event in the court's history because it gave juveniles almost all of the constitutional rights afforded adults.

Juvenile Court is presided over by three judges and two magistrates. The court's 23 probation officers supervise approximately 1,100 delinquent children at all times.

formally constituted court in what became the state of Colorado.

When Colorado became a state in 1876, probate jurisdiction was vested in the County Court and remained there for 88 years.

Two events significantly altered the court's operation. The first was the 1964 constitutional amendment which substantially reformed the structure of

bate and testamentary trusts, settlement of estates of deceased persons, appointment and supervision of guardians and conservators and the settlement of their accounts, as well as involuntary commitment for the care and treatment of mental illness and/or alcoholism. Outside Denver, this jurisdiction is vested in the district courts.

Denver Probate Court

Denver Probate Court traces its ancestry to 1855, when the Legislature of the Territory of Kansas passed an act creating the County of Arapahoe in the territory of Kansas; a county which encompassed virtually all of Colorado as we know it today. The same act gave the judge of probate, Allen T. Tibbits, authority to appoint all of the other initial county officers. This may have been the first

the Colorado court system. One part of that process was the creation by constitutional amendment of a new and separate Denver Probate Court. The second event was the adoption of the Uniform Probate Code in 1974. Colorado was among the first states to adopt the UPC, a statute that radically changed the probate process to one of simplicity and speed.

Probate Court has exclusive original jurisdiction in all matters of pro-

Members of the Denver District Court pictured are, from left to right: front row, Robert P. Fullerton, Larry J. Naves, Chief Judge John N. McMullen, J. Stephen Phillips, and Nancy E. Rice; middle row, Denver Probate Judge Field C. Benton, William G. Meyer, Federico C. Alvarez, Frank Martinez, Lynne M. Hufnagel, Edward A. Simons, Morris Ben Hoffman, and Herbert L. Stern III; back row, H. Jeffrey Bayless, Paul A. Markson, Jr., R. Michael Mullins, John W. Coughlin, Richard T. Spriggs, Connie L. Peterson, and Warren O. Martin. Not pictured is Robert S. Hyatt. Photo by Steve Zavodny

WESTERN AUTO SUPPLY
QUALITY and SERVICE AT A
DAVIS
AND
SHAW

SPOTLIGHT ON LEGAL SPONSORS

Denver, along with the rest of the country, rallied to support the First World War. The Denver Bar Association helped the cause by providing free legal advice to soldiers and their families. When the war ended a crowd of some 100,000 happy Denver citizens gathered along 16th Street to celebrate. Courtesy, Colorado Historical Society

Denver Bar Association

The Denver Bar Association has united, educated, and supported local attorneys and the Denver community for 100 years. The 6,000-member association is the oldest and largest local bar association in Colorado, with four of every five active lawyers registered in Denver County as members. Predating the formation of the Colorado Bar Association by six years, the DBA provides the means by which Denver lawyers contribute to their profession and to the public on a local level.

From the start the Denver organization campaigned for court improvement and worked to upgrade the profession. In the early 1920s it founded the Legal Aid Society and set up a law library which ultimately became part of the city's court system.

Today the Denver Bar Association is a volunteer, nonprofit service organization comprised of 25 committees. According to Jane Michaels, 1990-91 president of the Denver Bar Association, "The primary goal of the association is service— service to the legal community, service to the Denver community, and service to Colorado's indigent population."

Equal justice under law is the foundation of the United States' legal system, and the historic commitment of the private bar has been to keep that foundation solid. To that end, a group of DBA members established the Thursday Night Bar program in 1966. Its goal was to meet the growing need for volunteer legal assistance in Denver. In the 25 years since its inception, the TNB has become a model pro bono project and has expanded its services to benefit the surrounding metropolitan community as well.

Today the need for equal access to justice is more pressing than ever. The TNB is actively involved in several projects that address the special concerns of specific segments of the indigent population and others in need.

The TNB has forged strong alliances with other community service organizations. In cooperation with the Colorado AIDS Project, a panel of attorneys was recently established to address the legal needs of people with AIDS. In cooperation with the Denver District Court, the TNB initiated Family Law Court Week. The **biannual** clinic assists people with dissolution of marriage actions in Denver County. The program has been a huge success, and it is hoped that FLCW will expand its boundaries to include suburban counties in the near future.

The Denver Bar Association has been breaking ground in the legal community since its founding. Denver was the first large city in the nation to introduce Teen Court, and the second city in the nation to introduce the Early Neutral Evaluation concept into its court system.

Teen Court allows youths accused of committing minor infractions to be "represented" by their classmates and tried by a jury of their peers. Lawyers trained by Juvenile Court judges oversee the proceedings. The program has been so well-received that the DBA has hired a part-time staff member to coordinate the program with participating schools.

Early Neutral Evaluation (ENE) is designed to streamline complex litigation. It allows the district court judge to select cases to be referred to an experienced litigator who then serves as a neutral evaluator. ENE narrows the issues for trial, thereby speeding up the litigation process.

An educational partnership has developed between the bar and Denver schools, both public and private. The DBA Centennial coincides with the nation's Bicentennial for the Bill of Rights, and lawyers have teamed up with the Colorado Supreme Court and every school in the city to present an overview of this important document. The special program is devised to help students understand the significance of the Bill of Rights and its impact upon their lives.

Within the realm of public legal education, the DBA has developed numerous information services including the Call-A-Lawyer radio program, free clinics that address a variety of issues— among them pro se dissolution of marriage clinics, landlord/ tenant clinics, small claims/collection clinics, bankruptcy/foreclosure clinics—and the Tel-Law program.

One of the bar's most well-received volunteer programs has nothing to do with the law. The Friday Learning Hour is directed solely at the children of the homeless. DBA volunteers play games, help with projects, and read stories to the kids each week at The Gathering Place, a sanctuary for the homeless.

"One of the roles of the bar is to provide leadership and guidance to the legal community," says Michaels. Interprofessional committees and continuing legal education are hallmarks of the bar. The Young Lawyers Division is available

---

OPPOSITE: Past Presidents of the Denver Bar Association. Front row, left to right: Robert J. Kapelke, Garth C. Grissom, Donald E. Cordova, Miles C. Cortez, Jr. Maurice Reuler, Wesley A. Miller, Jane Michaels, William P. DeMoulin, William P. Cantwell, and Edwin S. Kahn. Back row, left to right: Richard P. Brown, Donald P. Mac Donald, Cathy S. Krendl, Bennett S. Aisenberg, Luis D. Rovira, Paul D. Renner, Royal C. Rubright, Leonard M. Campbell, William H. Erickson, Charles L. Casteel, and Willis V. Carpenter.

to any member under the age of 37. The Mentor program provides a one-on-one relationship between newly admitted lawyers and more experienced practitioners. The New Admittee program helps the

a journal concerning Colorado legal issues and developments in the field of law.

The historic fellowship between the bench and the bar is important to the DBA. Interprofessional

Promoting a greater sense of professionalism is one of the DBA's primary goals as it enters its second century. To that end, a Professionalism Committee was formed to look at what it means to be a lawyer, and

new attorney bridge the gap from law school to law practice.

Members keep abreast of key legal developments via two monthly publications: *The Docket*, a newsletter directed at the Denver legal community, and *The Colorado Lawyer*,

round tables are held regularly, where judges, lawyers, and public figures discuss law-related issues. In response to a request from Governor Roy Romer, the DBA helps evaluate judicial candidates chosen by the Judicial Nominating Commission.

issues surrounding lawyers' duties to clients, colleagues, and opposing counsel. Michaels says, "Our goal is to ensure that the practice of law in Denver remains of the highest caliber in competence, courtesy, and collegiality."

Morris & Lower

Images of eagles, hawks, and owls dominate the offices of Morris & Lower. From bronze sculptures on pedestals to oil paintings on the walls, birds of prey are everywhere—in flight, hunting, at the kill. Ask Bob Morris about the significance of all the raptors and he will say, "They hunt alone."

Bob Morris and Kathy Lower founded Morris & Lower in order to "hunt alone." They broke from a large Denver law firm in 1986 to establish their own practice, and today they have offices in both Denver and Vail.

At Morris & Lower there are no meetings and no employee handbooks; indeed, there are only two support employees. Modern technology makes Morris & Lower's streamlined operation possible. The firm is completely computerized, and its two offices are totally integrated, thanks to extensive telecommunications equipment.

The firm's lean, efficient lawyer and support staffing is designed to allow the two partners to do what they like to do—try lawsuits. A trial team since 1977, Morris and Lower like best to be in the courtroom, preferably in front of a jury. "Unfortunately," says Lower, "the justice system is oriented toward discovery, and that means that cases tend to take a long time to get to trial and become more complex than they need be. Large law firms thrive on this fact, and fortunately, as alumni of a large firm, we know how to deal with the wars of attrition that sometimes are waged against us."

The firm specializes in the areas of employment, business tort, breach of contract, and land use litigation. The majority of its clients are large corporations that are headquartered elsewhere. The firm acts only as defense counsel in employment disputes, but represents both plaintiffs and defendants in other types of litigation. Although Morris & Lower is now its own entity, the principals do not view themselves as an institution. "We see the firm per se as purely a means to an end, a vehicle to allow us to practice law with as little interference as possible from institutional concerns," says Morris.

The Morris & Lower philosophy is simple. "We want to be good lawyers, win lawsuits, make a living, and have fun if we possibly can—in that order."

ABOVE RIGHT: Bob Morris.

BELOW: Kathy Lower.

Clarke & Waggener, P.C.

Two diverse specialties, bankruptcy and family law, converged in a two-attorney practice when the law firm of Clarke & Waggener was founded in 1966.

The firm's first bankruptcy specialist, David J. Clarke, became a member of the Montana Bar in 1938 and a member of the Colorado Bar in 1946 under a rule permitting Colorado veterans who served in World War II to be admitted on motion if they were previously admitted elsewhere. Clarke had been with the Antitrust Division of the Justice Department in Denver when Pearl Harbor was bombed and reported the following week for active duty as a naval intelligence officer.

After service in China, he returned to the Antitrust Division in Denver in 1946, later transferring to the Atomic Energy Commission in Los Alamos, New Mexico, in 1948. He returned to Denver in 1951 as an attorney for the Wage Stabilization Board.

Clarke entered solo private practice in 1953 and concurrently served as a state representative from 1955 to 1957 and as a state senator from 1957 to 1961. He sponsored the Colorado Corporation Code and the Uniform Commercial Code. In recognition of his achievements, he received the Colorado Bar Association's Outstanding Attorney Award for 1965. A longtime Denver Bar Association activist, Clarke served as its president in 1971-1972.

In 1978 Clarke left the firm and resumed his government career in Washington, D.C., this time as a senior staff attorney with the Nuclear Regulatory Commission. He retired in 1986, 48 years after being first admitted.

In the meantime, the other half of the Clarke & Waggener practice was becoming an expert in family law. In 1963 William P. Waggener left a large Denver firm, which he had

ABOVE, LEFT TO RIGHT: Jon B. Clarke , William P. Waggener, David J. Clarke

joined in 1954, to go into practice by himself. For a time he investigated unemployment insurance fraud in Colorado, but he eventually came to specialize in family law, commercial litigation, and wills and estates.

Waggener began doing divorce work as part of his general practice. When he began practicing, handling divorces did not require a great deal of expertise, just common sense and an attempt to do what was fair and reasonable. However, in the past 10 years, divorce work has developed into a complex specialty, requiring a knowledge of current tax laws, child support guidelines statutes, Equity Retirement Act provisions, Former Spouse Protection Act provisions, and a host of other legislative enactments that impact custody, child support, maintenance, and division of marital property. Waggener keeps current by attending and/or participating and lecturing in family law seminars on a regular basis. In recognition of his expertise in the area of family law, he was elected as a Fellow of the American Academy of Matrimonial Lawyers in November 1976 and served as president of the Colorado chapter during 1989-1990.

Clarke and Waggener became partners in 1966 and engaged in general practice until April 1, 1973, when Chris Allison joined the firm. The Clarke, Allison & Waggener partnership lasted only five months, until August 26, 1973, when Allison died. Clarke and Waggener there-

after became a Professional Corporation. Between 1973 and 1983 a number of other attorneys were associated with the firm, including John W. Steinhauser, John M. Dudgeon, Anthony F. Renzo, Henry V.S. Hall, Joel Laufer, and Phillip J. Klint. In 1983 the firm left 17th Street and relocated in the Denver Technological Center.

After active duty as a naval aviator from 1965 to 1970, and after serving the firm as a law clerk from 1970 to 1972, Jon B. Clarke joined the firm as an associate attorney in 1973. He became a minority shareholder in 1978 and a 50 percent co-owner in 1983. He has followed in his father's footsteps as a bankruptcy specialist devoting full time to insolvency matters after 1978. He has represented a substantial number of Chapter 11 debtors-in-possession and operating trustees in reorganization proceedings before the United States Bankruptcy Courts in the District of Colorado as well as in other states. He also represents a number of entrepreneurs, executives, and professionals in individual Chapter 7 liquidation cases which have arisen following the failure of their businesses. He has been a frequent Continuing Legal Education faculty member on bankruptcy programs and is a member of the American Bankruptcy Institute.

Sheridan, Ross & McIntosh, P.C.

If the practice of law were to become obsolete tomorrow, the attorneys at Sheridan, Ross & McIntosh would have no difficulty starting new careers in different fields—most of them hold degrees in engineering or science. Mechanical, chemical, electrical, industrial, and aerospace engineers work for the law firm, as do organic and inorganic chemists, biochemists, mathematicians, and computer scientists.

Sheridan, Ross & McIntosh is the largest firm in the Rocky Mountain region specializing in the field of patent, trademark, and copyright law. Attorneys in the field require a scientific background because the nature of their specialty often involves protecting new technology. A comprehensive understanding of complex scientific concepts is essential to representing clients, whether that client is a research geneticist patenting a new discovery or a multinational corporation protecting its equipment design. Sheridan, Ross & McIntosh attorneys are called upon to perform a tightrope act: daily balancing the practicalities of the law and an in-depth knowledge of technical subject matter.

"TMs are the words and symbols used to distinguish the goods and services of one company from another, and are frequently one of the most valuable assets of that company," says Michael McIntosh, senior partner. Trademark protection may often require relatively little in the way of legal services, but failure to properly protect this asset can result in costly litigation or the loss of rights.

Sheridan, Ross & McIntosh has extensive experience in the area of domestic and international trademark registrations. The firm provides a comprehensive search service through in-house databases

to determine the availability of tradenames and trademarks. The firm also assists the marketing and advertising departments of a company to ensure that its marks are used properly and consistently. It provides a watch service for potentially conflicting trademark and service mark applications and uses by competitors.

The trademark attorneys of Sheridan, Ross & McIntosh together represent nearly a century of experience in the various aspects of trademark law.

Sheridan, Ross & McIntosh does not operate as a collection of individ-

ual practitioners, but as a unified professional team, functioning in a vertically integrated fashion. The senior attorney in the firm most qualified to meet the specific requirements of a particular company assumes direct responsibility and accountability to that company and its legal coordinator. The senior attorney is then assisted by appropriate legal specialists in accordance with the needs of each project. The international department works with qualified associates throughout the world to counsel clients concerning decisions related to international patent and trademark matters. A trademark op-

position and cancellation team protects the rights of clients through vigilance and, if necessary, challenges to national and international trademark registrations or applications. The contracts group covers all facets of patent and trademark transfers, including licensing, assignments, negotiations, and drafting of the necessary documents. A specialized litigation team works exclusively in the field of patent, trademark, copyright, trade secret, and unfair competition law. All efforts are monitored by SR&M's managing director.

Founded in 1952, the firm grew substantially during the 1980s.

It has achieved and maintained what McIntosh calls "critical mass." The firm is sufficiently large and diversified to meet the scientific requirements of its clients, but remains capable of operating with maximum communication and coordination between its members and the companies they serve.

Technology has helped the firm achieve its objectives. It developed its own computer and software system to manage its resources and provide detailed accounting of ongoing work. In addition, the firm subscribes to worldwide patent and technical databases in order to re-

main current with relevant scientific advances.

McIntosh says that technology is important to the operation of the firm, but that the focus of the practice is still the client. "We exist for the sole purpose of assisting the companies with whom we work to accomplish their missions," he says. "We're here for them. We strive to ensure that the companies we represent are competitive within their industries."

Michael McIntosh says for all intents and purposes, the small inventor who makes millions from a high-tech component he designed in his garage is just a romantic notion today. As a general rule, the successful modern inventor is backed by solid management and adequate capital. "It's a sophisticated game today," says McIntosh. "One that requires total commitment and tactical resourcefulness from the outset."

Sheridan, Ross & McIntosh helps companies "play the game" by evaluating all issues associated with proper ownership and title in a particular technology, while at the same time considering the viability of trade secret protection. The firm conducts investigations for companies to determine the scope of their possible operation without violating the legitimate rights of others. This is accomplished through in-house patent searches by attorneys well versed in the literature and using comprehensive databases.

SR&M provides a unique resource to the region and to the clients it serves. It has grown and diversified to reflect the needs of the region's companies and continues to evolve and expand in anticipation of the ever-increasing sophistication required to assist the companies with whom the firm serves.

Patrick C. Hyde, P.C.

Patrick and Martha Hyde consider the practice of law the most rewarding opportunity to combine their talents and help people. Their practice combines Patrick's international background with Martha's labor and real estate background. The practice started as a general civil, business, and litigation practice largely extending legal services to Colorado's Spanish-speaking population. The firm also acted as corporate counsel to a family construction corporation.

Patrick's international education started in 1968 and enabled him to become fluent in Spanish, German, and French. He has now practiced law and translated legal documents in all three languages. He enhanced his international interests by focusing on international business and immigration law classes in law school. After law school he volunteered and translated legal documents for the Catholic Immigration Service, and interpreted in the Denver courts for the Justice Information Center. He also volunteered services to the Colorado Foreign Trade Office, the state office which advises local businesses how to export their products. He is now teaching federal government contract law at Lowry Air Force Base, and he has written student manuscript materials for U.S. Department of Defense personnel.

Martha entered law school with a real estate and labor background. After law school she worked as an attorney for the U.S. Department of Labor, a negotiator for the Union of Flight Attendants, and as an attorney in Colorado Springs practicing personal injury and workers' compensation. Recently she has concentrated on the areas of personal injury, workers' compensation, real estate, wills and estates, and bankruptcy.

One reason for the firm's growth and success is its diversified character. This character was exemplified after Congress passed the Immigration and Control Act of 1986. Patrick made several public service appearances in Spanish on local Spanish radio stations to assure that the Hispanic community was aware of the newly created rights. He encouraged his clients to fight for family unity under the law, which they eventually won in the form of the U.S. Immigration family fairness policy. The practice has branched out to help this clientele resolve other legal entanglements as well.

Martha and Patrick Hyde

The practice has not only offered immigration services to individuals, but has also served international corporate clients, helping them acquire business immigration visas. The practice is gradually gaining more international clientele.

The firm's philosophy is based upon a love for justice. The firm's goal is to make affordable legal services available to all.

Banta, Hoyt, Greene & Everall

Ask Richard J. Banta what events or developments over the past 30 years have been significant factors in shaping the law firm of Banta, Hoyt, Greene & Everall, and he will say without hesitation: "The growth of the southeast metropolitan area."

The view from his Greenwood Plaza office bears witness to the validity of this assessment. Office towers have replaced barn-wood farm buildings and six-lane highways have all but erased memories of rutted dirt roads.

Banta, Hoyt has been associated with, and located in, the greater southeast Denver metropolitan area since the 1950s and is the result of a 1976 merger of two separate prominent law firms. The firm moved from its long-established Englewood offices to its present location in 1985. Since Banta, Hoyt was directly involved in substantial governmental and private activities leading to the expansion of the southeast metro area, the move was a logical expansion of the firm's practice.

A general practice firm, Banta, Hoyt's longevity in the southeast community contributed to its emphasis in municipal, special district, education, real estate, and commercial law. The surge in population and commercial growth in the southeast Denver area brought with it the need for expanded educational facilities and water, sewer, and electrical services.

For more than 25 years Banta, Hoyt has provided legal services to the area's school districts, assisting them in the acquisition of school sites and in the development of educational facilities and services necessary to meet the demands of a more than 400 percent growth in student population.

During the last quarter-century Banta, Hoyt has also been actively involved in the development of special municipal and quasi-municipal districts to develop and provide water, sewer, and other municipal resources for the community, and in the expansion of electrical services for residential and commercial customers of a large multicounty electrical utility involved in the wholesale purchase and retail sale of electricity.

Since 1953, when one of the firm founders, Richard L. Banta, Jr., first served on the Englewood City Council and subsequently in the Colorado Legislature as a state representative, members of the firm have participated in local and state political, governmental, and professional activities. Banta served as the first president of the Arapahoe County Bar Association when it was organized in 1958 by a handful of local attorneys, including firm member Richard D. Greene. This organization has since grown to more than 300 members with other past and present members of Banta, Hoyt. Val Hoyt and Richard Greene have both served as its president.

The members of Banta, Hoyt have been designated as attorneys for several municipalities, including the City of Englewood, Greenwood Village, and the towns of Platteville, Gilcrest, and Johnstown. Two of the firm members have been former

Firm founder Richard L. Banta, Jr.

deputy district attorneys for Arapahoe County.

Adding to their influence in the community, the members of Banta, Hoyt have served in various capacities for numerous organizations and community boards. Richard L. Banta, Jr., served on the Colorado State Highway Commission for eight years; Hoyt and Banta have served as members of the Swedish Hospital Board of Trustees; Hoyt has served as attorney for and president of the Centennial Chamber of Commerce; and Greene served 10 years as a district court judge in the Eighteenth Judicial District.

Banta, Hoyt has grown with the community it serves and presently has a staff of 24, including the firm's 12 attorneys. Richard J. Banta predicts the southeast metropolitan area will continue to grow, although more slowly and more solidly than in the recent past. The future goal of Banta, Hoyt, Greene & Everall is to continue to expand its practice to accommodate the challenges of the future development of the community with which it has grown.

Firm shareholders left to right: Charles A. Kuechenmeister, Richard D. Greene, Darryl L. Farrington, Jane B. Garrow, and Richard J. Banta.

Welborn Dufford Brown & Tooley, P.C.

Since its founding in Denver more than 30 years ago, Welborn Dufford Brown & Tooley, P.C., has pursued quality, integrity, and professionalism in the practice of law. Its commitment to these values has earned the firm an enviable reputation in Denver's business and legal community.

Although it has experienced steady growth over the years, the quality and stability of its practice has been more important to the firm than size. It was founded in 1960 by Robert Welborn and Philip Dufford, who brought together respected backgrounds in the fields of corporate and natural resources law. Today Welborn Dufford Brown & Tooley, P.C., has more than 25 lawyers, and

Left to right: Thomas G. Brown, Robert F. Welborn, and Philip G. Dufford.

S. Kirk Ingebretsen (seated) and Gregory A. Ruegsegger.

more than half of its attorneys are also shareholders.

Welborn Dufford has a broad-based business and litigation practice, and is nationally known for its work in the natural resources field of law, including water, oil and gas, and mining. Its clients, many of whom have been clients of the firm for years, are diverse, reflecting the firm's experience and expertise in many fields of practice. These clients include manufacturing companies; retailing companies; oil and gas, mining, and energy related companies; banks, financing, and leasing companies; software firms; health care organizations and medical groups; real estate development entities; governmental and quasi-governmental entities; railroads; and farming and ranching organizations.

Effective representation of clients in these areas requires proficiency in a wide range of areas, including corporate mergers and acquisitions; antitrust; antidumping; financing; taxation; general corporate matters; environmental law; bankruptcy and workouts; labor; public utilities; condemnation; international transactions; federal and state securities matters; legislation; litigation and trial practice; alternative dispute resolution; products lia-

bility; personal injury and workers' compensation; water law; and mining and oil and gas law.

The firm is experienced in all phases of litigation, including trials and appeals in federal and state courts, as well as hearings before federal and state administrative agencies and arbitration panels. Cases tried range from complex commercial and natural resources disputes to personal injury and constitutional matters, as well as complicated bankruptcy proceedings. In that regard Welborn Dufford has represented the Colorado legislature in a variety of constitutional law cases.

Recognizing that litigation is both expensive and time consuming, the firm is committed to minimizing the impact of litigation on its clients. To that end, it is an advocate of the various alternate dispute resolution procedures. In keeping with that objective, the firm is a supporting member of the Center for Public Resources, a New York-based organization dedicated to promoting alter-

Left to right: Gerald Padmore, Thomas G. Brown, David W. Furgason, and Marla E. Valdez.

native dispute resolution, particularly in the context of commercial conflicts.

The firm also has extensive experience in the area of environmental law. Its work in that area began in the 1960s and it continues today on all levels—local, state, and federal. In addition to handling specific matters involving air and water quality, hazardous waste, and CERCLA, the firm has been extensively involved in legislation and regulatory rule-making concerning those matters. It has also been involved in litigation concerning insurance coverage for environmental liabilities.

In recent years the firm has increased its international practice. Business transactions, mining ventures, property interests, manufacturing, contracting, and other legal matters have been handled both for American firms doing business outside the United States and for multinational enterprises and other foreign firms in either the United States or other countries. The firm has represented clients in transactions occur-

Left to right: Richard L. Fanyo, Beverly J. Quail, William C. Robb, and Kathryn L. Powers.

ring in the USSR, the Republic of Korea, Germany, Italy, Japan, Australia, Liberia, Brazil, and several other countries. In keeping with this effort, one of the firm's shareholders, who is originally from Liberia, is actively involved in representing the growing interests of various clients of the firm in relation to natural resources and other projects in Africa.

To maintain its place in Denver's competitive legal environment,

Welborn Dufford focuses on serving its clients faithfully and well. Believing that this can best be done by people of broad perspective, the lawyers of the firm are also active, visible leaders in the legal and business community. Some have served as president of the Denver and Colorado Bar associations. Others hold positions of leadership on boards of nonprofit community organizations. Still others are involved in governmental affairs and public service. One shareholder of the firm served on the Colorado Court of Appeals. Another served as dean of the University of Colorado School of Law. Still another is a past chairman of the Colorado Oil and Gas Conservation Commission. Others have taught at various law schools. The firm also encourages all of its employees to contibute their time and talent for the benefit of the community, whether at the local, state, or national level, and whether in the form of pro bono legal work or other activities beneficial to society in general. In so doing, the firm as a whole continually grows and stays in touch with the many forces and concerns that affect the lives and businesses of its clients.

Welborn Dufford Brown & Tooley, P.C., begins the decade of the 1990s with highly qualified lawyers. It enjoys a practice rich in diversity and growing to meet the demands of new areas of business, as well as the needs of its clients in an environment that is experiencing major changes, both locally and abroad. It is a firm that continues to command respect for its unfaltering foundation of integrity and commitment to excellence in the practice of law.

Grant, McHendrie, Haines & Crouse

Grant, McHendrie, Haines & Crouse was created in Denver in 1926 as Grant, Ellis, Shafroth & Toll. The four attorneys who founded the firm were as colorful as the era.

William W. Grant was the nephew of James D. Grant, one of the first governors of Colorado. W. W. Grant loved the law. He felt a deep sense of civic responsibility and concern about national affairs and politics. He made an unsuccessful run for mayor of Denver in 1933, and was at one time considered for an Undersecretary of State post under Woodrow Wilson. The outspoken attorney was a strident opponent of the Ku Klux Klan, an unpopular stance at the time. He also advocated United States military involvement in World War II prior to the Pearl Harbor bombing, an equally unpopular view. After the United States entered the fight, Grant was awarded the Order of the British Empire for his service before the war.

Erl Ellis was one of the leading mining attorneys in Denver. A civil engineer and naval aviator, Ellis had a passion for Western history and wrote five books and numerous published articles on the subject. He was called "a human landmark in Colorado legal and historical circles" by Colorado historian Tom Noel. Ellis gained notoriety as one of the trio who bugged Governor Teller Ammons' office in 1937. Ellis, a staunch Republican, said he "eavesdropped" on the Democratic governor to "detect any wrongdoing that might be planned by high state officials." Because there was no state law against eavesdropping back then, the three conspirators were convicted of a nuisance and Ellis was required to post a peace bond for one year. He returned to practice after his brief sabbatical and continued practicing into his eighties.

Morrison "Morrie" Shafroth became involved in Democratic politics while offering campaign support for his father, "Honest John" Shafroth, then governor of Colorado. In 1936 Franklin D. Roosevelt appointed the younger Shafroth as Chief Counsel of the Bureau of Internal Revenue, a post he would fill during World War II. In 1937 he was ordered by Secretary of Treasury Henry Morganthau to produce the federal income tax returns of Andrew Mellon (Hoover's Secretary of Treasury) and other prominent and wealthy individuals. Shafroth refused, believing such disclosure to be a violation of individual privacy. He was thereupon called to the White House and informed by the president that he must either testify and produce the returns or tender his resignation. His resignation was on the president's desk the next morning.

The *New York Times,* in an editorial under the headline of "Courageous Resignations," stated, in part: "There are not too many men in public life who are willing to give up

Erl Ellis, one of the founders of Grant, Ellis, Shafroth & Toll.

Peter J. Crouse, senior director of the firm.

that, in 1967 to the Western Federal Building, and in 1983 to One United Bank Center, where it was one of the first tenants.

One of the firm's early clients was the Atchison, Topeka & Santa Fe Railway Company for Colorado, a client Ellis brought with him to the firm. When Ellis left his father's firm to form Grant, Ellis, Shafroth & Toll, his father passed the railway account on to his son. The firm has spent a great deal of time working with the State Public Utilities Commission on a variety of railroad and utility matters. The all-purpose law firm soon became recognized for its expertise in railway litigation.

Grant, McHendrie's work on

major construction litigation has had a significant impact on state development projects, including the Eisenhower Tunnel and Blue Mesa Dam & Reservoir. When the brand new Clay Creek Dam spilled over its sides in 1965, Grant, McHendrie's task was to prove that faulty construction had caused the massive flood. Eight years and several scale models later, the firm proved its case.

Today the firm specializes in a variety of commercial, real estate, and natural resources transactions, as well as complex commercial litigation, but the practice alters to accommodate changing needs. The firm is expanding its governmental practice as businesses face increased and multiple levels of government regulation.

Grant, McHendrie is a small firm by today's standards, but regularly handles cases with and against much bigger firms. The firm has appeared hundreds of times before the Colorado Supreme Court. "Grant, McHendrie is the best small firm in Colorado," says President Keith Tempel. Senior Director Peter Crouse concurs. "It's nice practicing in a firm this size. It's flexible and versatile. Plus, we can be as structured as we need to be or as loose as we want to be."

More than half of the directors, and nearly that number of associates, have spent their entire legal careers at the 65-year-old firm. "I guess the true legacy that has been handed down through all the years is loyalty, and the simple fact that people love to work here," says Crouse.

their jobs for the sake of principle, and Mssrs. Shafroth and Ryan deserve public gratitude for the dignity, decency, and courage of their action."

Henry Wolcott Toll may be best remembered for founding the Council of State Governments. The Colorado state senator also was an archenemy of the Ku Klux Klan. In 1925 the KKK obtained and secured control of the Colorado legislature. Toll was one of six members of the Colorado Senate who refused to meet with the Klan-dominated Republican caucus. Despite threats to him and his family, he successfully moved to block the Klan's program.

Between 1927 and 1967, the firm operated out of the Equitable Building, moving just twice after

Keith Tempel, president and managing director of Grant, McHendrie, Haines & Crouse.

Montgomery, Green, Jarvis, Kolodny & Markusson

None of the three lawyers who founded Montgomery, Green, Jarvis, Kolodny & Markusson practiced law a single day in Colorado before they hung up their shingle here. Michael Montgomery, Keith Jarvis, and James Green founded the firm in 1984, shortly after moving to Denver. Dennis Markusson and Joel Kolodny signed on a few years later.

All five attorneys were involved in the biggest toxic tort litigation the nation had ever seen. Before they moved west, Montgomery, Jarvis, and Kolodny practiced at a major Virginia law firm that represented the Johns-Manville Corporation in its asbestos litigation. During that time, Markusson and Green were Johns-Manville's corporate counsel.

Montgomery came to Colorado on business in 1983 to continue his efforts in pursuing the government for its share of the asbestos damages. While here, he, Jim Green, and Keith Jarvis met and discussed their mutual desire to open a Denver trial practice. Their desire became reality on April 1, 1984, when they opened the office of Montgomery, Green & Jarvis in the Denver Tech Center.

The firm was launched at the end of the oil boom. Montgomery recalls that from the windows of their offices they could see nine construction cranes busily erecting new buildings. When the firm moved downtown one year later, only one crane remained.

"When we opened shop, we had two clients—Johns-Manville Corporation and Dow Chemical Company," Montgomery says. Shortly thereafter the firm became Colorado products liability counsel for Coca-Cola.

Kolodny joined the firm in 1987, bringing with him considerable insurance and products liability expertise. Markusson, a nationally recognized expert in toxic torts, came aboard in 1988.

"We were able to develop a significant client base in a short period of time in part because of the diversity of our combined litigation experience," Green says. "Our goal was to build on that experience to develop a balanced litigation firm." While all had experience in the relatively new field of toxic tort litigation, each individual also possessed prior experience in a variety of fields, including products liability, insurance, environmental, and professional malpractice. Their combination of backgrounds as in-house counsel and private practitioners served to further balance the firm.

Today Montgomery, Green, Jarvis, Kolodny & Markusson engages primarily in civil litigation, with an emphasis on personal injury claims, products liability, environmental claims, EPA Superfund litigation, and insurance coverage. With the exception of commercial litigation, the firm's practice is defense oriented.

And firm oriented. "We are a firm," Montgomery says. "When you hire us, you get the firm. We refer to ourselves as 'we.' We don't view ourselves as a group of lawyers who just happen to practice law together."

The firm's five senior partners from left to right: Dennis H. Markusson, C. Michael Montgomery, Joel A. Kolodny, H. Keith Jarvis, and James K. Green.

The Women's Bank

As recently as the 1970s, women were denied credit and loans in their own names. Women applying for a loan had to have their husbands, ex-husbands, or even fathers cosign their notes.

The Women's Bank was founded during the height of the feminist movement. Forty-nine women and one man invested $1,000 each to bring banking services to minorities and women. "We approached this as a business, not a social crusade," says Judi Wagner, president of the founding association.

The board sought a national charter to circumvent resistance in the state regulatory system to a so-called "feminist" bank. This also allowed the bank to automatically qualify for F.D.I.C. insurance.

Mary Roebling, who in 1936 was the first female bank president in the United States, joined the group

One of the bank's past board of directors. Seated left to right are: Wendy Davis, Barbara Sudler, Leslie Davis, Gail Schoettler, Lorrie Norgren, and Beverly Martinez-Grall. Standing left to right are: Edna Mosley, Steve Shraiberg, Betty Freedman, Jack Stern, Judith Wagner, LaRae Orullian, Joy Burns, Verner Averch, Jean Yancey, and Paul Howes.

LaRae Orullian, the current chair and chief executive officer of the Women's Bank.

as chairman of the board. Her clout made a significant difference in obtaining a national charter, which was granted on July 7, 1977. The charter enabled the board to recruit a qualified president and chief executive officer, LaRae Orullian.

While the federal Equal Credit Opportunity Act of 1975 abolished some obstacles between women and credit, discrimination pervaded the banking industry itself. Although 70 percent of bank employees were women, less than one percent were in senior management positions. Orullian was part of that one percent.

She started work as a bank messenger after high school and worked her way up from coin wrapper to executive vice president. At one time or another she has held every position in a bank—except teller. Currently the longest serving bank president on 17th Street, Orullian is proud of being the first female bank president in Colorado. She is even prouder that she now shares the title with 23 other women.

Orullian came aboard the Women's Bank in 1977. She, Wagner, and an assistant spent the next year writing the prospectus and selling 100,000 shares in the bank. All 100,000 shares were sold to 800 local residents within six months, without the help of an underwriter.

The Women's Bank opened its doors July 14, 1978. First day deposits totaled one million dollars. "We turned a profit immediately," Orullian says. "The financial goals we set for the first 12 months were met within 12 weeks."

Among Colorado financial institutions, Women's Bank ranks near the top in fiscal strength as measured by standard industry profitability ratios. The bank's position is so sound that it is frequently requested to bid on insolvent financial institutions being liquidated by federal regulators.

Orullian credits the bank's success to its policies, personnel, and high standards. "If someone is turned down for a loan, we explain what it takes to get approved the next time around. Customers tell us that the word in the community is, 'If you can get a loan at the Women's Bank, your business must be solid.'"

Bruce C. Bernstein, P.C.

One of the most significant evolutionary changes in the operation of a law office is the addition of non-attorney administrators. Generally only large firms employ professional management personnel, but Bruce Bernstein, a sole practitioner, is the exception. As Bernstein's business manager, Anne Rocheleau is responsible for client and practice development, personnel, public relations, and finance. And he is responsible for practicing law. "Because valuable attorney time is not sacrificed on administrative matters, we are able to keep our prices competitive while offering individualized attention to the client," says Rocheleau.

The firm's practice has been shaped by Bernstein's unique back-

Bruce Bernstein, a New York native, has made his home in Colorado since 1964. He was graduated with honors from the University of Denver Law School in 1970.

ground. He served for three years as the executive director of the Legal Center for Handicapped Citizens and continues to represent physically and mentally challenged individuals with special education placement, employment rights, guardianships, Social Security disability, and zoning for group homes. He often assists personal injury attorneys in structuring settlement agreements to protect assets and maximize services to persons handicapped by their injuries.

Bernstein was one of the first Colorado lawyers to become a member of the National Academy of Elder Law Attorneys. Elder law is a natural outgrowth of handicapped law because many elderly persons share similar needs for residential placement and Medicaid funding. Bernstein is knowledgeable in estate planning and can advise clients in the orderly management of assets, taking into account the eligibility requirements for Medicaid and other needs-based social programs.

The firm has an active bankruptcy practice, representing individual and corporate debtors, creditors, and panel bankruptcy trustees. Bernstein's own background as a panel trustee for the United States Bankruptcy Court from 1980 to 1990 provides him with a compre-

hensive understanding of bankruptcy laws and procedures.

The final area of emphasis is family law. "I am occasionally asked whether I am aggressive or whether my manner is conciliatory," says Bernstein. "I emphasize that my responsibility is to fully advise clients of their rights and options so that we can jointly identify and prioritize goals and determine how aggressively to pursue them. In dissolutions involving small children, the desire to maintain positive communications with the other parent is often paramount." Rocheleau's training in mediation and arbitration enables her to assist clients choosing one of these avenues of dispute resolution as an alternative to the courtroom.

In addition to direct client representation, both Bernstein and Rocheleau are authors of published articles and frequently speak to business and nonprofit organizations on their respective areas of expertise.

Bruce Bernstein and Anne Rocheleau at the firm's offices at 925 East 17th Avenue in Denver. The converted Victorian residence was originally built in 1896 by Frank Edbrooke, the architect best known for designing the Brown Palace Hotel.

Bradford Publishing Company

LEFT: The Bradford-Robinson Printing Co. at 1824 Stout Street in Denver, circa 1916. The building was located across the street from the U.S. Post Office.

BELOW: The company's building remained at the same address in 1947 but expanded and updated its appearance.

Bradford Publishing Company publishes legal forms and other publications pertaining to Colorado law for the Colorado legal, financial, and real estate communities. It also distributes the *Colorado Revised Statutes* and related publications.

Less than a century ago, legal forms were manufactured individually to meet specifications defined by individual law firms. When a firm needed a will or lease form, a printer was commissioned to create the form. It was an expensive and labor-intensive process. In the late 1800s a printer named W.F. Robinson calculated that he could save everyone time and money by producing standardized legal forms.

The legal forms sold by Bradford Publishing Co. today are those originally published by W.F. Robinson as *Robinson's Legal Blanks*. Robinson, an early employee of the *Rocky Mountain News*, founded the W.F. Robinson Printing Co. in 1881. In 1905 Daniel W. Bradford and two partners founded the Bradford Publishing Company. In 1916 Rollie W.

Bradford purchased the W.F. Robinson Printing Co. and established the Bradford-Robinson Printing Co., which eventually became the largest printer in Denver. When Robinson and Bradford merged, the Bradford Publishing Co. took over publication of the legal forms.

The forms publications business evolved through need. In 1935 the Bradford-Robinson Printing Company began to publish statutes for the State of Colorado. It continued to do this until 1953, when the

state decided to recodify the statutes. At that time it set up the Office of Revisor of Statutes, and the state published the statutes itself. From 1953 to 1963 the statutes were printed in Chicago. In 1963, when the statutes were again revised, the Bradford Publishing Company won the contract to compose, print, and distribute them. Bradford was awarded the contract a second time in 1973.

Bradford Publishing Co. has been serving the Rocky Mountain region since 1881 as the largest publisher of legal forms. "We continually endeavor to keep our library of more than 1,000 forms current, accurate, and readily available," says chief executive Brad Bradford. "We engage the services of attorneys who specialize in keeping our forms revised in accordance with legislative acts, court decisions, and the needs of the legal, financial, and real estate professions."

Bradford Publishing Co. markets primarily by direct mail, dispatching more than 30,000 catalogs a year. A well-known Denver landmark, the company was located across from the post office for 50 years, until it moved into a renovated warehouse at 1743 Wazee Street in 1988 as part of a drive to revitalize lower downtown. In 1989 the company won the Historic Denver, Inc., Award of Honor for its historic contribution to the city it has called home for nearly a century.

West Publishing Company

Throughout its history West Publishing Company has analyzed, edited, indexed, and published over 3 million court decisions. Each year it adds approximately 130,000 new decisions to that total.

It all started in 1870, when 18-year-old John West moved with his parents and brother to Minnesota and secured his first job as a traveling salesman for the D.D. Merrill Book Store. He found that the lawyers he visited were chronically hindered because they had to wait weeks or months for court reports and other practice books to arrive from the East.

In 1872 West left the bookstore and established himself as Minnesota's first full-time law book salesman. Under the title, John B. West, Publisher and Bookseller, he sold law treatises, dictionaries, and office supplies, and traded in new and used court reports. He also sold a fairly complete line of legal forms.

John's older brother, Horatio West, brought his business acumen to the company in 1876. The brothers soon commenced publishing a weekly pamphlet called *The Syllabi*, under the name John B. West & Company, which contained excerpts from the decisions of Minnesota courts. The first issue covered the Minnesota courts solely in excerpt fashion, but very soon the Wests were publishing the full text of the decisions of the Minnesota Supreme Court.

In early 1877, just six months after it was begun, *The Syllabi* was replaced by the weekly *North Western Reporter*, the forerunner of the modern West reporters, containing decisions from Minnesota and Wisconsin courts. Two years later this publication was replaced by a new series of the *North Western Reporter*, which published the full text of all current decisions from Iowa, Minnesota, Michigan, Nebraska, Wisconsin, and the Dakota Territory. Within three years the *Federal Reporter*® and the *Supreme Court Reporter*® followed.

After 1885 the West Publishing Company (as it was incorporated in 1882) added four reports to its roster which, along with its current reporters, gave the courts nationwide coverage.

Official reports, processed through the state, were often years old by the time they reached the practicing bar. John West designed the National Reporter System® to collect and arrange in an orderly manner in the shortest possible time the material every judge and lawyer must use, thus safeguarding the doctrine of stare decisis.

The National Reporter System® was a resounding success. Lawyers received the

BELOW: West Publishing Company was incorporated in 1882. The company's first president was John B. West (seated at left), who served 17 years. Horatio D. West (standing at right) succeeded his brother as president and served until 1908. He was succeeded by Charles W. Ames (standing at left), who held the position until 1921. Peyton Boyle (seated on the right) was the company's first editor-in-chief.

BELOW RIGHT: An editorial office, circa 1926. The editor, one of the 40 employed at the time, studies opinions received from courts across the nation, and dictates points of law and a summary containing the salient points of each case.

PUBLISHED WEEKLY,
By John B. West & Co.,
60 W. Third Street, ST. PAUL, MINN

Terms $3.00 per annum in Advance.

Rates of Advertising.

Spa.	1 w.	2 w.	3 w.	1 w.	3 m.	6 m.	1 y.
1 Sq.	.75	1.30	1.90	2.15	6.00	11.65	22.50
2 Sq.	1.50	2.60	3.60	4.50	11.80	22.50	41.25
3 Sq.	2.10	3.75	1.90	6.00	17.25	33.00	65.25
½ C.	2.65	4.70	6.15	7.50	21.50	41.25	81.50
1 C.	5.00	9.00	11.80	14.45	42.40	81.80	162.25

1 sq. consists of one inch of the column.

John D. O'Brien   Homer C. Eller

O'BRIEN & ELLER,
ATTORNEYS AT LAW,
Ingersoll Block. ST. PAUL. MINN.

WARREN H MEAD   CYRUS J THOMPSON
MEAD & THOMPSON,
ATTORNEYS AT LAW,
Cor. Third and Wabashaw Sts., St. Paul.

Special attention given to Bankrupt Proceedings and Collections. Loans securely placed

W. P. WARNER,
LAWYER,
Cor. Jackson and Fourth Sts., Hale's Block.
SAINT PAUL, MINN.

Jas Smith, Jr.   James J Egan

SMITH & EGAN,
ATTORNEYS & COUNSELORS AT LAW,
SAINT PAUL. - MINN.

SESSION LAWS.

We have the Session Laws of Minnesota from 1849 to 1875 inclusive, 34 vols., which we offer in sets, or by the volume.

Parties wishing to fill their sets, will do well to send list at once

The syllabi of the decisions of the Supreme Court of Minnesota have heretofore appeared in the daily papers only as it happened to suit the convenience of a reporter, or when a scarcity of news made them useful in filling up space, sometimes being in one paper, and sometimes in another.

It has been a matter of much annoyance to the attorneys of our State that these decisions have not been published regularly in some one paper, immediately after being filed, and well knowing the importance of such a publication to the profession, we propose issuing the "Syllabi."

It will contain the syllabus, (prepared by the Judge, writing the opinion,) of each decision of the Supreme Court of Minnesota, as soon after the same is filed as may be practicable, accompanied, when desirable to a proper understanding of the points decided, with an abstract of the case itself, and when the decision is one of general interest and importance, with the full opinion of the Court.

It will also contain abstracts of, and opinions in the more important decisions in the United States Courts of Minnesota, as well as those of particular interest decided in the several District Courts of the State. The general design being to furnish the legal profession of the State, with prompt and reliable intelligence as to the various questions adjudicated by our own Courts, and at a date long prior to the publication of the regular reports.

It is not our purpose to confine our attention exclusively to reports from our own State, but while making those first in importance, also to furnish digests or opinions in cases decided in other States, which may have a special importance here or be of more than general interest.

New law books will be noticed as they appear.

We shall endeavor to make the Syllabi indispensable to Minnesota Attorneys, by making it prompt, interesting, full, and at all times *thoroughly reliable*, and the better to enable us to do so we respectfully request the cordial support of the members of the Bar.

JOHN B. WEST & Co.,
Publishers.

John West's first publication, The Syllabi, *was an eight-page weekly news sheet that contained "prompt and reliable intelligence as to the various questions adjudicated by our own courts at a date long prior to the publication of the regular reports." The first edition was published Saturday, October 21, 1876.*

Designed by St. Paul architect J. Walter Stevens, this building was completed in 1887 and located on the side of a bluff facing the Mississippi River. The building was eight stories high, but only three were visible from the street side.

texts of court decisions in a matter of weeks— not months—and the reports were relatively inexpensive.

But lawyers were still swamped by decisions. West's solution was the American Digest System®, which indexed court decisions through headnotes and key numbers, allowing users to find information in the National Reporter System®. With the creation of the digest, it no longer mattered how voluminous court reports became—the American Digest System® provided lawyers with convenient access to them. Used together, the West "systems" made it possible for lawyers to find reported decisions from their local jurisdiction, as well as from state and federal courts across the country.

The innovative company didn't rest on its laurels, however, and in 1908 West began publishing its well-known American Casebook series for law schools that used actual cases as models. In 1927 West published the *United States Code Annotated®*, the first annotated federal code. In 1936 West took over publication of *Corpus Juris Secundum®*,

the United States' most comprehensive encyclopedia of law.

The company next ventured into the statutes publication field. For over 50 years West has been producing statutes with editorial enhancements, providing a road map for attorneys to find case law interpreting a statute section. Today West publishes annotated statutes in 21 states, and thousands of new statutes and annotations are added yearly. The first *Colorado Revised Statutes Annotated* became available in 1990.

Legal research hasn't been the same since the development of computer-assisted legal research in the 1970s. West introduced WESTLAW®, its computer-assisted legal research service, in 1975. Cases can be online almost as fast as the judges file them with their clerk of court. U.S. Supreme Court cases are generally on-line within one hour. Today the more than 2,000 databases available on WESTLAW cover statutes, court decisions (full text plus headnotes and synopses), administrative law, texts, and periodicals.

CD-ROM technology was computerization's next wave, and West quickly adapted the technology's unique characteristics to attorneys' needs. Each disc in West's CD-ROM Libraries™ can store the equivalent of 300,000 typed pages, putting entire collections of specialized legal and tax materials on a desktop. Lawyers can search for material just as they would on WESTLAW, but because they have the discs at their disposal, they can take their time perusing the collection.

In 1989 West Publishing Company expanded its printing and binding facilities into a 31-acre

plant in Eagan, Minnesota. The company has grown from a one-person operation in 1872 to an expanding business with more than 3,700 employees in 1991. West publishes some 55 million books and pamphlets yearly—more than 20 billion pages.

By early 1992 West will have completed the move of its corporate headquarters from St. Paul, Minnesota, where it has been located since 1872, to Eagan, Minnesota, the present 31-acre site of its printing, binding, and warehouse facilities.

West Publishing and its employees take pride in being "forever associated with the practice of law." President and Chief Executive Officer Dwight D. Opperman says, "Partially through our efforts our country's laws are applied more evenly and justice is meted out more quickly and fairly. We know that the freedoms all Americans enjoy are better protected because of the work we do each day."

West Publishing Company has had only eight presidents in more than a century of doing business. Dwight D. Opperman, current president and chief executive officer, took over October 18, 1968.

Gelt, Fleishman & Sterling P.C.

Gelt, Fleishman & Sterling P.C. was formed on the basis of the individual strengths of each of its founding partners, Theodore Z. Gelt, A. Craig Fleishman, and Harry M. Sterling. Founded in January 1989, the firm brings together expertise in the areas of tax, estate and business planning, commercial, construction, injury, professional liability litigation, debtor-creditor rights, workouts, and bankruptcy. The firm has developed one of the region's leading tax practices, which frequently confronts unique and innovative taxation issues. All of the firm's tax lawyers hold either Masters of Taxation degrees or are licensed as Certified Public Accountants. Because of their expertise in tax specialization, Gelt, Fleishman & Sterling attorneys frequently serve as consultants and expert witnesses to other attorneys.

Harry Sterling is a nationally recognized attorney authority in all phases of debtor-creditor relations. He began practicing in the bankruptcy court in 1958. With more than 30 years bankruptcy law experience, Sterling has become a highly regarded expert who lectures on the subjects of debtor-creditor and bankruptcy law at the University of Denver and the University of Colorado. As the first chairman of the Bankruptcy Rules Committee, he has particular insight into the practice methods in the Bankruptcy Court for the District of Colorado. Sterling is a recognized expert witness in bankruptcy matters and court proceedings.

Theodore Gelt has practiced law in Colorado since 1975 and has special expertise in the area of taxation. His practice focuses on providing clients with expert and innovative guidance for major corporate transactions, tax planning, estate planning, business planning, and real estate. Gelt is a past chairman of the Taxation Section of the Colorado Bar Association. He is also a member of the Executive Committee of the Rocky Mountain Region of the Anti-Defamation League.

Craig Fleishman's practice emphasizes commercial, construction, professional liability, lender liability, bad faith, and insurance litigation. A nationally known expert in professional liability matters, he is a frequent national and local lecturer, and is a contributor to *Legal Malpractice, 3rd Edition*. Fleishman is chairman of the Colorado Bar Association's Professional Liability Insurance Committee and also serves as a column editor for *The Colorado Lawyer*.

The firm blends its tax and estate planning expertise to design the most tax-efficient structures for the conservation and preservation of business and personal assets. Gelt says, "We strive to balance flexibility with the degree of complexity appropriate for each individual client's estate planning objectives." The firm's bankruptcy department has extensive experience in workouts and bankruptcy from the debtor, trustee, and creditor perspectives.

Gelt, Fleishman & Sterling also specializes in defending professional liability claims involving lawyers, hospitals, brokers, accountants, and other professionals. "The license and reputation of a professional are his or her greatest assets," says Fleishman, "and the firm aggressively represents professionals who have been sued for malpractice."

Financial institutions, as well as current and former officers and directors of both banks and savings and loans, are frequently represented by the firm. Remedial and preventive advice is routinely provided to clients in the areas of director and officer liability, as well as development of prudent operational systems to minimize the potential of claims or suits.

The firm feels that contributing to the community is part of each firm member's duty to enhance the quality of life for others. Members are encouraged to teach and write on matters of interest to attorneys as well as members of the public, and the firm has worked to raise funds for cancer research, to promote religious and ethnic tolerance, and to enhance health care.

BELOW: Theodore Z. Gelt

BELOW CENTER: A. Craig Fleishman

BELOW RIGHT: Harry M. Sterling

Lockton Silversmith, Inc.

The Lockton Insurance Agency merger with J.H. Silversmith, Inc., in 1989 brought together two of the top locally owned insurance agencies in the Rocky Mountain region to form Lockton Silversmith, Inc. Silversmith has been a name in Denver insurance since 1895, and the Lockton Insurance Agency was founded in Kansas City in 1966 by Jack Lockton. Lockton Silversmith, Inc., has since become the most prestigious broker in Denver. With more than 400 associates and nearly $40 million in revenue in 1990, Lockton is one of the largest insurance brokers in the United States.

Today the issues surrounding lawyers' liability are so complex that for most law firms the purchase of this coverage has become a major decision. Lockton Silversmith, Inc., has developed a professional liability unit that has the ability and experience to handle the intricate insurance needs of law firms.

Nationally recognized in the United States and London as an expert on lawyers professional liability coverage, Sharon C. Oliver, vice president of the Professional Liability Unit, provided more than one-third of all policies for Colorado's lawyers. She joined Lockton Silversmith in 1990 because of the tremendous support and resources available at the agency. "My ability to handle complex matters on behalf of my clients increased tenfold when I joined this organization," she says.

Oliver first began working with professional liability coverage in 1978, and rapidly became Colorado's premiere authority in the field. The issues are significant and complex, but Oliver's vast reservoir of experience allows her to solve her clients' problems quickly, economically, and effectively.

"Fifty percent of the lawsuits against lawyers nationally result from a failure in their administrative sys-

ABOVE: Standing, left to right: William O'Connell and Joseph Silversmith. Seated: Sharon C. Oliver.

RIGHT: Jack Lockton

tems," she says. To protect against such failures, Oliver developed an audit program which allows firms to identify potential problems. Lockton also designs custom loss control programs using a systematic approach that identifies exposures and risks inherent to the firm's operation.

Oliver was instrumental in developing a risk management strategy and continues to identify areas of importance to Colorado's lawyers. A frequent speaker at continuing legal education seminars, she is also active in the legal community as an Associate Member of the ABA's Standing Committee on Lawyers Professional Liability. She is a former member of the Board of Directors for Colorado Lawyers for the Arts and a Colorado Bar Association committee member. Oliver also served as director of the Profes-

sional Liability Underwriting Society.

Oliver calls herself a professional working for professionals. "We look out for our clients in the way they look out for their clients. I care about my lawyers—I'm not driven to sell an insurance product, but to help them meet their insurance needs."

Davis, Graham & Stubbs

Davis, Graham & Stubbs celebrated its 75th anniversary at a former crack house in the heart of metropolitan Denver. The attire was decidedly understated for a diamond anniversary celebration; old blue jeans and hard hats were the dress of the day. Members of the firm ate cold sandwiches and drank ice water as they gutted interior walls and tore out ancient plumbing. The party ended at dusk and cost the firm $100,000.

The money and labor were donated to help convert an abandoned duplex into a Montessori preschool and daycare center for low-income families. With the help of various agencies, Family Star Infant Parent Education Center opened its doors early in 1991. But the grand opening did not signal an end to the firm's involvement with the project. Volunteers from the firm continue to work with neighborhood families on housing, employment, and consumer problems. Others do landscaping and maintenance at the center.

A committee of Davis, Graham

An inner-city crack house was converted to a child-care center, as volunteers continued the firm's commitment to community service. Courtesy, Rocky Mountain News

& Stubbs employees, faced with the prospect of organizing a gala 75th birthday celebration, recommended the donation in lieu of other festivities. The firm embraced the idea and an ongoing commitment to the project. "Making a [cash] contribution is too easy to give and too easy to forget," says Jim Bunch, managing partner. "You give money and then say, 'Alright, I've done my part.' The community has been very good to us over the years, and we thought it would be appropriate to give something back."

Indeed, Davis, Graham & Stubbs itself might not exist today if not for the charitable acts of others. The firm was founded in 1915 by James Benton Grant and Mason Avery Lewis under the name of Lewis & Grant. In 1917 the two founders were called to serve their country in World War I. The fledgling law firm almost certainly would have perished in their absence, but for the efforts of Tyson Dines, senior partner of Dines, Dines & Holme. Dines volunteered to handle the Lewis & Grant practice until the principals returned from war.

Upon their return, Dines handed them detailed reports of all the work he'd done in their absence and all the fees he'd collected on their behalf. "I love that story," says Donald S. Stubbs, senior partner. "It

Mason Avery Lewis (left) and James Benton Grant founded the firm in Denver in 1915.

The firm had its beginnings in Denver's newest and tallest office building in 1915. Courtesy, Denver Public Library, Western History Department

epitomizes the quintessence of professionalism in this or any field."

The early Lewis & Grant days were spent securing clients. One of the firm's largest accounts was the Denver National Bank, which the firm represented on a retainer arrangement at a fee of $2,500 per year. The second retainer client was Henry Van Schaack. The firm later became counsel for the Prudential Insurance Company, the W.H. Kistler Company, and the Boettcher family interests.

After World War I the law practice of Lewis & Grant grew significantly. By the early 1940s the firm had four large corporate accounts: the Denver National Bank, the American Crystal Sugar Company, the Potash Company of America, and the Colorado Milling and Elevator Company.

Lawyers prominent in this early firm included Albert Craig, the first associate of Lewis & Grant; Frederick Sanborn, Jr.; Irving Hale, Jr.; and J. Ramsay Harris.

Robert L. Stearns became an associate with the firm in 1920. He later became dean of the University of Colorado Law School and president of the University of Colorado. Stearns was of counsel to Davis, Graham & Stubbs until his death in 1977.

Richard Marden Davis became an associate with the firm in 1936. Davis had been roommates with Quigg Newton throughout preparatory school and Yale, and the two friends had always hoped to become law partners. After graduation from Yale Law School, Newton accompanied William C. Douglas to Washington, where Douglas headed the Securities and Exchange Commission.

Newton joined Lewis & Grant as an associate in 1937. He worked on SEC registration statements and also on certain aspects of the reorganization of the Denver & Rio Grande Western Railroad. During that same time period, Davis worked for two years doing abstracts with Fred Sanborn and Irving Hale, as well as tax work with Stephen Hart.

Quigg Newton and Richard Davis became brothers-in-law in 1935 when Davis married Nancy Newton. Three years later the brothers-in-law left Lewis & Grant to become part-

ners in the firm of Newton & Davis on the second floor of the Colorado National Bank Building. The firm started with one client—the University of Denver, which paid a retainer of $75 a month.

Newton & Davis did extensive SEC work and established the Founders Mutual Fund and the Dow-Theory Fund, the first mutual funds in Denver. The firm also did extensive labor work with the National Labor Relations Board.

In 1940 Donald S. Graham, who had been teaching at the University of Colorado Law School, joined Lewis & Grant. Two years later Don Stubbs, who was practicing law in Montrose, Colorado, joined the firm. Graham and Stubbs also became brothers-in-law in 1947 when Don Graham married Lucile Stubbs.

In 1947 the two firms (Newton, Davis, Drinkwater & Henry and Lewis & Grant) merged, after James Grant died and Quigg Newton was elected mayor of Denver. The new firm name was Lewis, Grant, Newton, Davis & Henry. In 1952, after Arthur Henry left and it became clear that Quigg Newton was staying

Richard M. Davis (1912-1987) served as president of the Denver Bar Association, 1959-1960.

Donald S. Graham (left) and Donald S. Stubbs continue to keep the firm's philosophy and values alive with their active participation in firm affairs.

in public life, the name of the firm was changed to Lewis, Grant & Davis.

Byron R. White, who had joined the firm in 1947, left in 1960 to be appointed deputy attorney general by President John F. Kennedy, and two years later Kennedy appointed him to the U.S. Supreme Court. Mason Lewis retired in 1961 and died in 1963. After his death, the firm changed its name to Davis, Graham & Stubbs.

The name of the firm changed a number of times over the years. Less noticeable than the name changes were the evolving philosophical changes. Two of the major philosophical changes centered around the firm's growth and its civic involvement. Lewis & Grant favored limited growth. By contrast, Davis, Graham & Stubbs has chosen to expand. The firm, which began with two partners in 1915, had grown to more than 180 lawyers in 1990.

The growth of the firm has stayed abreast of the growth of Denver and Colorado, both in terms of population and significance to the economic and financial development in the Rocky Mountain region. "If you want people to feel like there is a future for them in the firm, you have to make it big enough so there is somewhere for them to go," says Donald W. Hoagland, a senior partner who joined the firm in 1951. There are certainly places for members to go today. The firm currently has offices in Denver, Salt Lake City, and Washington, D.C.

Davis, Graham & Stubbs expanded into Washington, D.C., in 1979, largely to better serve its clients in the natural resources area. Over time the Washington office has gained a much broader focus, including a thriving international practice.

The other significant philosophical difference between the firm then and the firm today is that, "Neither Lewis nor Grant took part in bar association activities or other community involvement, and both abstained from political involvement," Stubbs says. "Davis, Graham & Stubbs, on the other hand,

Former partner Byron White was appointed to the United States Supreme Court by President John F. Kennedy in 1962.

encourages its attorneys to engage in civic activities." George Hopfenbeck managed the initial, successful campaign of John Love, Republican candidate for governor. Dick Freese managed the first successful campaign of Dick Lamm, Democratic candidate for governor. "Both had the support of the firm," says Stubbs.

Davis, Graham & Stubbs lawyers have actively participated in community affairs, serving as directors of such organizations as Mile High United Way, the Denver Art Museum, the Denver Symphony Orchestra, the Colorado Commission on Higher Education, the Colorado Association of Commerce and Industry, and the Greater Denver Chamber of Commerce.

Service to the legal profession has been a priority for many of the firm's lawyers. Don Stubbs served in many capacities in the Denver and Colorado bar associations and became president of the Colorado

Bar Association during 1974-1975; Don Graham was elected to membership in the American Law Institute in 1946; and Dick Davis was president of the Denver Bar Association in 1960, a position also held by Charles Casteel in 1988-1989.

The firm has also developed a strong tradition of pro bono professional work. "I have always felt that lawyers who involve themselves in human problems of the community are better lawyers. There is a risk that lawyers in a large firm . . . become people who only know how to draft complicated pieces of paper. They miss some of the substantive context and content a person with broader human experience might catch," says Don Hoagland, for whom the Colorado Bar Association's Donald W. Hoagland Award for pro bono work is named.

While the firm experienced philosophical evolution, the practice of law was also changing. Don Stubbs

A meeting of the firm's executive committee. From left: Dale R. Harris, Barbara Pierce, James T. Bunch, Donald J. O'Connor, and Lester R. Woodward.

and Don Graham agree that the biggest change in this area was the development of a need for specialization. Prior to World War II, the firm was a general practice firm and the only area of specialty was the income tax department.

The firm soon began to han-

Clients and employees enjoy the firm's comfortable working environment.

dle numerous SEC and labor relations matters. The increasing demand for natural resources led to other specialties. "Water law has always been important and new issues come to the forefront daily," Graham says. Today the firm has 13 distinct practice groups and provides a full range of services to its clients.

Davis, Graham & Stubbs survived two world wars, the Great Depression, and 75 years of social, political, and technological change. It was only fitting, then, that on its 75th anniversary, the firm celebrated its past with an investment in Denver's future.

Harding & Ogborn, P.C.

Harding & Ogborn, P.C., descended from a longtime Denver and national firm, Nelson & Harding. Nelson & Harding was founded in 1953 by J. Max Harding and Bob Nelson in Lincoln, Nebraska. Harding was with the Public Service Commission and Nelson was with the Attorney General's Office when they decided to fulfill their mutual dream of building a transportation/trial practice.

The motor carrier industry was heavily regulated by the federal government in the 1950s. Thus, Nelson & Harding had an extensive practice catering to businesses who wanted to obtain operating authority, and conversely, catering to those which wanted to oppose businesses attaining that authority. The firm's early reputation was based on its representation of contract carriers and small, entrepreneurial truck lines.

During the 1960s and 1970s the firm expanded its services to include corporate law, management labor matters, personal injury and products liability, and mergers and acquisitions work. At the height of its practice, the firm had 75 attorneys in seven offices across the United States.

The Denver office of Nelson & Harding opened in 1971 and focused its efforts on corporate law and real estate matters. The firm continued its involvement in the transportation industry, but in 1980, when the federal government changed the regulatory scheme altogether, that involvement decreased. While it continued to represent carriers in matters at the state level, the firm's involvement at the federal level was limited to business consulting. The firm began doing more business with shippers, and more merger and acquisition work in the trucking industry.

In 1989 Nelson & Harding merged with a national law firm. The new firm dissolved in early 1990 and affiliates went in all directions. Attorneys from the original group of Nelson & Harding offices in Lincoln and Denver rose from the ashes to form Harding & Ogborn on February 17, 1990. Harding & Ogborn is headed by William A. Harding and Murray Ogborn. The firm specializes in labor, litigation, corporate, and tax estate planning, as well as a significant transportation practice.

Murray Ogborn says, "In general, the people who practice law here do so as a team at every level. There is no hierarchy; it is a total team effort on behalf of our clients. We approach each case by putting our best people on it. In this complex world, any significant problem is multifaceted, and multifaceted problems require a teamwork approach."

Harding & Ogborn has a national practice that is centered in Lincoln, Nebraska, and Denver, Colorado. "This firm is truly a firm for the 1990s," explains Ogborn. "We began with a focus on dedicating ourselves to our clients' needs and getting the job done. We believe that by keeping our attention on details and by listening more than talking, we can continue to carry out our goal of best representing our clients' needs."

Murray Ogborn

William A. Harding

Holt & Associates, A Professional Corporation

Entering the beveled glass French doors that lead to the offices of Holt & Associates, at 900 Penn Center in the Capitol Hill area of Denver, one is immediately immersed in an alluring, almost exotic environment that hints of a law practice far from the ordinary or traditional. An artistic African sculpture—assembled of entwined, wooden parts—rests on a marble coffee table in the waiting room. A bronze five-piece jazz ensemble sculpture facing the office entrance conveys a vibrancy and energy amid a

L. Tyrone Holt, president and founder of Holt & Associates.

pleasant yet strong interplay of pastels, greens, and mauves. While dynamic and intriguing, the mood is also modern, orderly, and tasteful.

Holt & Associates is a law firm that consistently expresses the genius of boldness. Founded in 1983 by Tyrone Holt (who made the conscious decision to identify and serve the needs of the modern business economy), this firm has developed a reputation primarily through its strong and competent handling of complex and multiparty litigation of product liability, management labor,

accounting, and construction industry cases. Additionally, many of Colorado's major architects, engineers, and builders in the construction industry look to Holt & Associates for counsel regarding contract negotiations, professional liability, legislative, regulatory, and insurance matters.

The firm represents clients in the United States District Court for the District of Colorado, the Tenth Circuit Court of Appeals, the Colorado Supreme Court, the Colorado Court of Appeals, and in the various trial courts throughout the state of Colorado. It has extensive pretrial and trial experience in virtually all regions of the state.

The firm is predominantly engaged in defense work and the representation of corporate and business clients. All of the firm's attorneys are litigation specialists. The firm has managed a host of consumer products lawsuits as well as cases involving bridge and other structural collapses, subdivision foundation problems, and automobile mechanical system failures. Clients range from architectural, engineering, and health care firms to airline carriers and public utilities to manufacturers in the mining, food, and toy industries.

Holt & Associates is one of Denver's largest minority-owned-and-operated law firms. An entrepreneurial spirit is a significant part of the firm's philosophy, capitalizing on organization, discipline, and sensitivity to clients' objectives and needs.

Late in 1989 Holt & Associates identified business opportunities in the state of Colorado and the Rocky Mountain region which made apparent the need to develop skills for the

This five-foot-high bronze sculpture of three proud Masai warriors, standing back to back and looking out in all directions, is symbolic of Holt's three-sided approach to running his firm.

practice of public finance law. On June 1, 1990, Holt & Associates became affiliated with Lewis, White & Clay (a Detroit law firm with a highly regarded national practice in the area of public finance) to form a business relationship for the specialized practice of public finance law to be known as Lewis, White, Clay & Holt.

In 1977 Lewis, White & Clay became the first predominately African-American firm listed in the *Directory of Municipal Bond Dealers of the United States* as bond counsel. Lewis, White, Clay & Holt will be listed in the upcoming edition of The Buyer's *Municipal Marketplace* as bond counsel. Lewis, White, Clay & Holt is sure to distinguish itself with outstanding performance in the public finance area.

Tyrone Holt, president of the firm, is known as a skillful, hard-hitting, and dynamic trial lawyer. A 1974 graduate of Stanford University School of Law, Holt completed his undergraduate degree at Morehouse College and undertook further studies at the University of Ghana in West Africa and the University of Madrid in Spain. Prior to founding Holt & Associates, he worked with a major law firm in Denver.

Active in the Attorney's Arbitration/Mediation Center in Denver, Holt is committed to alternative dispute resolution as a way to save clients both the time and expense involved in litigation. He is both an arbitrator and mediator for the American Arbitration Association.

As a frequent lecturer and seminar orchestrator, Holt is regarded by groups that include the National Convention of the Construction Specification Institute, the Association of Civil Engineers, the State of Colorado Chapter of the American Institute of Architects, the American Society of Civil Engineers, and the Society for Marketing Professional Services as an authority in the areas of design, professional, and insurance law. He is active in government relations and was recently nominated as chairman of the Colorado Bar Association Litigation Council.

Internally, Holt manages his firm with the same kind of vitality and

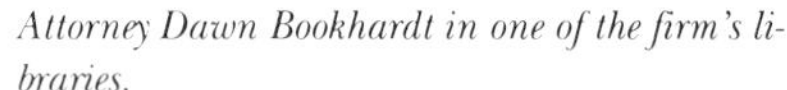

Attorney Dawn Bookhardt in one of the firm's libraries.

A bronze five-piece jazz ensemble sculpture facing the office entrance contributes to the firm's dynamic atmosphere.

charisma that he demonstrates to the public. An African sculpture located at the entrance to his office reinforces Holt's disciplined, versatile, and innovative approach to the practice of law. The five-foot-high bronze sculpture of three proud Masai warriors, standing back to back and looking out in all directions, is symbolic of Holt's three-sided approach to running the firm, an essential part of its success.

This three-sided approach involves the effective internal interaction of the three facets of the firm's work force: management, attorneys, and support staff. Each is considered equally important. Each provides a different perspective to serving clients, and each guards both the firm's and clients' interests from a different vantage point.

The African decor is a theme carried out in Holt & Associates' offices and intensifies the firm's spirit, energy, and personality. Emphasizing a team approach to work, the firm likens itself to the hardworking and noble Masai warriors, a faction of an African tribe whose members live on the open plains of the Great Rift Valley in eastern Africa. Originally from Kenya, the Masai are disciplined hunters, experts at war, and known for their intelligence, bravery, adaptability, and loyal yet independent spirit.

An atmosphere of cooperative diversity—a phrase coined by Holt— permeates the firm. Cooperative di-

Innovating a problem-solving approach.

versity, explains Holt, closely describes the firm's "constant exchange of ideas, a cross-section of perspectives, a commitment to professionalism, and a modern approach to the law that emphasizes results for clients. The variety of backgrounds, talents, and ideas provided by our staff leads to innovative problem solving."

Attorneys of the firm are young, dedicated, energetic, and success oriented. Many came to work at the firm immediately after graduating near the top of their law classes, from schools that include the University of Denver College of Law, Gonzaga University, and Boston University.

At Holt & Associates, the team approach to client problems is emphasized and carried out. Attorneys view legal problems as opportunities and develop answers through brainstorming and constant interaction—designed to add strength to the firm's ability to serve its clients. Two attorneys are always assigned to each case.

Diane Andy, Holt & Associates' human resources manager, explains that all employees are given as much opportunity for growth as they can handle. Bureaucratic layers, typical of larger organizations, are virtually nonexistent at the firm. Instead, focused, creative thinking is stressed and expected. While Holt guides the attorneys, they are also given the chance to grow and experiment.

Dawn Bookhardt, an attorney who joined the firm after graduating from the University of Denver College of Law, says, "Holt & Associates allows me to infuse my own creativity into the practice of law. The firm is nontraditional in the sense that it is open to the concept of young associates flourishing. Bold thinking and achievement are always encouraged. We are truly warriors in that we become highly experienced in handling conflict."

To Kevin O'Toole, another attorney, the cooperative, caring, and almost family-like attitude among the staff is what makes Holt & Associates unique. "This cooperation and respect combines our energies for synergistic and effective results," he remarks.

The firm's modern approach to business is demonstrated in its commitment to becoming a paperless office. The firm uses state-of-the-art computerized systems ranging from time-saving legal word-processing programs to the use of electronic messages and mail.

Holt & Associates not only stresses disciplined and creative thinking, but also cares about the physical well-being of its staff. The image of the tall and strong Masai warriors, who need to be in top condition to survive and thrive, is constantly present. In 1989 the entire firm began an exercise and nutrition program under the guidance of personal trainers who measured each employee's body fat, blood cholesterol count, and fitness levels. Individual programs were then developed for physical enhancement and stress reduction.

Holt & Associates is ambitiously looking ahead to the future by preparing itself for a period of continued growth and expansion. It is dedicated to a modern, entrepreneurial approach to business.

In 1860 Dr. Ludwig Krapf published the first known written description of the Masai warriors in his book, *Travels, Researches and Missionary Labours.* "They are dreaded as warriors, laying all waste with fire and sword so that the weaker tribes do not venture to resist them," wrote Krapf. More than 100 years later, Krapf's words are illustrated by Holt & Associates in its attitude and outlook.

Holt confers with a secretary on document preparation.

Vinton, Waller, Slivka & Panasci

The law firm of Vinton, Waller, Slivka & Panasci was created on August 1, 1990, when two established Denver firms merged—Waller, Mark & Allen, P.C., with Vinton, Slivka & Panasci. The merger resulted in a consolidation of talent between seasoned veterans in litigation and banking from both firms. The "new" firm has years of experience in numerous state and federal courts at the trial and appellate levels, as well as in arbitration, administrative hearings, and other proceedings.

"Our sole purpose for being here is to provide quality legal service to our clients," says William Waller, Jr. The 11-member firm specializes in complex civil and criminal litigation, banking and financial institution regulatory law, and tax and corporate law. It represents a broad range of clients, including individuals, trusts and estates, government entities, and businesses and financial institutions. Corporate clients range in size from one-person operations to some of the largest banks and securities firms in the world.

The group handles many different kinds of complex litigation cases. The firm represented a multibillion-dollar out-of-state bank in its capacity as trustee for mortgage bond revenue programs and served as cocounsel for the defense in a complex commodities fraud action that was one of the largest fraud cases ever decided in Colorado. The firm also defended a municipality in a $15-million suit against the town based on allegations of antitrust violations and other constitutional claims.

The firm's two banking and bank regulatory law partners, Robert Vinton and Ernest Panasci, perform the bulk of the firm's banking and regulatory practice. The firm has been involved in scores of bank acquisitions and bank and thrift failures/acquisitions in recent years. Vinton, Waller, Slivka & Panasci represented an applicant in a two-year effort in structuring and gaining approval in 1987 for the first commercial bank ever chartered in the United States whose services are devoted exclusively to children.

The firm's principals, with more than 100 years of collective experience in the legal profession, have observed dramatic changes in the practice of law. Technology has been the catalyst for many of the more recent changes. William Waller points out that as late as the 1970s, law firms still used carbon paper, there were few national law firms in existence, and all of Vinton, Waller, Slivka & Panasci's clients were from Colorado.

Today the firm represents numerous national and international clients with the aid of technologies such as satellite transmissions, facsimile machines, and computers. But as much as the changes in the legal area are accelerating, says Waller, "there will always be lawsuits; it's the way those disputes will be handled that will change. I think we should direct our energies toward defining issues and presenting evidence in as complete and economical a manner as possible."

The firm's six partners, pictured left to right: Robert M. Vinton, William C. Waller, Jr., Kevin D. Allen, Ernest J. Panasci, Richard P. Slivka, and Denis H. Mark.

Calkins, Kramer, Grimshaw & Harring

Calkins, Kramer, Grimshaw & Harring helped build Colorado from Douglas County to Steamboat Springs. In large part, Denver's southeast business corridor exists as it does today because of the firm's efforts. It also provided all of the legal services required for the planning and development of Highlands Ranch and created many of the state's special districts.

The firm encompasses five major categories of practice, including corporate, municipal law and finance, real estate and land use, natural resources, and litigation. It

Harold H. Calkins (1916-1991)

represents both residential and commercial real estate developers and facilitated the construction of ski resorts like Vail, Purgatory, Breckenridge, and Steamboat Springs from the ground up. In fact, there was only one building, an old tool shed, in the area now known as Mt. Werner before it was built into a major ski area. The tool shed served as the meeting place to decide whether or not to build the ski resort. The first bond issue for the development of Mt. Werner at Steamboat was $100,000. "Things have gotten considerably more complicated—and expensive—since then," says Tom Grimshaw. "Today that sum wouldn't buy the postage."

Calkins, Kramer works with local and out-of-state clients in virtually all matters related to the creation and maintenance of special districts. It represents more than 100 of Colorado's special districts, many of which were organized by the firm.

Calkins, Kramer has been instrumental in drafting legislation that governs real estate and special districts. Members of the firm have served in various capacities with the state, as staff director to the State Land Use Commission and as members of the Legislative Drafting Office. Former state legislator Tom Grimshaw (1967-1970) served as chairman of the State Housing Board. Because of these and other associations, the firm was involved in the drafting and litigation of a significant part of the state's current land use laws.

The practice covers all areas of natural resources law, including water law, water quality, public land law, oil and gas, coal transportation, taxation, and environmental law. The firm has developed water supplies for clients with projects in both urban and outlying areas.

It is not only Colorado that has undergone profound change. The operation of a law office has changed significantly through the years and the firm's founders note a greater emphasis on management today than ever before. "When there were six or seven of us together, we held management meetings by shouting down the hall," recalled the late Harold Calkins, one of the founding partners.

Like the business of law, the financial community is also evolving. Legislation and regulation are breaking down the traditional distinctions between savings and loan associations, banks, and brokerage houses, placing new demands on the firm's clients as well as creating new opportunities for them.

Patten, McCarthy & Associates

Since 1980 Patten, McCarthy & Associates has offered professionals a resource for simplifying business operations in today's complex economic environment.

Les Patten and Jayne McCarthy founded Patten, McCarthy & Associates to fill a gap in the banking industry—the demand for objective, expert analysis of every facet of operating a financial institution—and wound up filling financial needs in other industries.

The firm has provided financial institutions with in-depth economic and financial analysis to determine the impact of proposed mergers or acquisitions. It is frequently called upon to mitigate the risk involved in managing a loan portfolio, a critical task in any economic environment. The firm has become expert in pro-viding valuations and analyses of tangible and intangible assets for accounting, tax, and regulatory purposes.

"We offer something an accounting firm can't offer," says Les Patten. "We're almost an engineering firm in the technical sense." The two principals gained their technical expertise working in the trenches at financial institutions. Both were officers at a large, successful Denver bank prior to launching Patten, McCarthy & Associates. Patten served as president and chief operating officer, and McCarthy was vice president and controller.

The firm's expertise in the financial arena allowed it to easily branch out into other commercial territories. "First and foremost we are a consulting firm," says Patten, "but more than 30 percent of our business is dedicated to litigation support."

Patten, McCarthy & Associates gained invaluable experience in the area of litigation support while working with clients' legal counsel in providing expert testimony in complex business litigation. The firm has provided testimony regarding the interpretation of financial data, has reconstructed financial activity, and has assisted with bankruptcy reorganization plans and asset valuations.

The firm is frequently called on to calculate damages. It has assisted in the application of the tax code and prepared analyses in support of taxpayer positions.

As Certified Fraud Examiners, Patten, McCarthy & Associates provides organizations with an analysis of internal controls and systems to aid in the prevention of fraud. The firm is expert at investigating suspected fraud activities.

Patten, McCarthy & Associates is often retained to provide business solutions to professional corporations. Corporations engaged in the practice of law know that it is becoming increasingly competitive, and clients are becoming increasingly sensitive to fees. Patten, McCarthy & Associates has devised a law practice operational audit to identify ways of increasing the amount of cash available to the owners of law practices.

The audit evaluates the efficiency of, and control over, cash management practices; identifies opportunities for increased efficiency via automation; assesses the effect of current compensation and benefit plans on productivity; and reviews the firm's strategic business planning and practice development techniques.

Every enterprise, whether it is established or just getting started, can benefit from an objective review of its business methodology. Those who are serious about success make Patten, McCarthy & Associates a regular part of their planning process.

Jayne McCarthy and Les Patten

Holland & Hart

Since 1947, when Steve Hart and Joe Holland left established Denver practices to form a new law firm, Holland and Hart has remained committed to two concepts: To help the clients achieve their goals by providing the highest quality legal services in a prompt, professional, and ethical manner, and to maintain a profitable and satisfying work environment.

Stephen Harding Hart and Josiah G. Holland and their associates, William D. Embree, Jr., and Peter H. Dominick, founded the firm on July 1, 1947. Jerome L.J. Hart, Stephen Hart's older brother, joined the firm as a partner a year later, in 1948. The founding members had a number of traits in common which enabled the young firm to establish its place in a booming post-war community. They shared cultivated minds, a love of the West, family traditions of professional service, highly competitive natures, and a commitment to the community beyond the firm's doors. They admired hard work and performed it.

In the early years, the firm's lawyers specialized in mining, corporate finance, and taxation, but soon found opportunities in oil and gas, as well as other sub-specialties which now fall under one or more of the firm's three departments: Business, Natural Resources, and Litigation.

Holland and Hart's business practice represents the concerns of businesses throughout the region, serving clients in traditional areas as well as in newer specialities pertinent to the taxation and regulation of Western and national industries. Holland & Hart, now 240 lawyers strong, has adopted a regional focus that allows the firm to offer its regional and national clients legal problem-solving skills wherever their interests take them, with offices in Boise, Idaho; Billings, Montana; Cheyenne, Wyoming; Aspen, Denver,

Joe Holland

The Denver Tech Center, and Colorado Springs, Colorado; and Washington, D.C.

The client work in natural resources arose from the businesses which grew in the Rocky Mountain region. Mining, oil and gas, and water practices developed into regulatory and environmental specialities as the federal government increasingly governed the vast resources-rich Rocky Mountain region and prompted businesses to respond to

Steve Hart

Jerry Hart

related concerns.

Litigation was at the heart of the firm's original practice. Joe Holland was at home in the courtroom, while Steve Hart's favored habitat was the legislative back room, or the 17th Street board room. Holland and Hart's trial practice began in the traditional areas of antitrust, tax, labor, and real estate. These areas have since spawned highly specialized practices which reflect changes in the manufacturing and business communities, such as advanced technology and intellectual property.

As the Denver legal market matured, the firm's emphasis on client service has become a source of continuing pride. The concept is an ongoing reality today, from managing partner to messenger. The lawyers and staff at Holland and Hart keep clients' needs at the focal point of their work.

Holland and Hart has always been active in pro bono, community involvement, and service to the profession, exemplified by dedication to a broad range of pro bono legal work, civic, and bar activities. One especially memorable pro bono contribution was made by Steve Hart, the first State Historical Preservation Officer, who is cred-

ited with saving downtown Denver's central landmark, the Daniels & Fisher Tower. In 1988 Holland and Hart was the first law firm to receive the Donald W. Hoagland Award for exceptional pro bono service, and in 1989 the firm received the Colorado Lawyers Committee annual award for outstanding contribution to the cause of civil rights under the law.

As it enters its fifth decade, Holland and Hart is looking toward a new century of serving clients in the Rocky Mountains, across the nation, and around the world.

Kirkland & Ellis

Kirkland & Ellis is one of the largest law firms in the United States and one of Denver's prominent law firms. Founded in 1908 by Colonel Robert McCormick, grandson of financier Joseph Medill, owner of the *Chicago Tribune*, the firm generated a Chicago and Midwest-based corporate client list to rival the leading New York firms.

With offices in Chicago, Washington, D.C., Los Angeles, New York, and Denver, Kirkland & Ellis represents some of the largest national and multinational corporations throughout the United States and abroad. The firm's rapidly expanding client list includes manufacturing, sales, and service corporations, investment banking firms, real estate lenders, financial institutions, and trade associations.

The Denver office opened in 1981. Despite the economic downturn of the mid-1980s, the office has experienced remarkable growth. It has increased tenfold from four lawyers in 1981 to more than 45 attorneys today.

The firm's growth and success is a result of its operational system—a meritocracy. Webster defines meritocracy as "an education system whereby the talented are chosen and moved ahead on the basis of their achievement."

Kirkland & Ellis operated on much the same basis as other law firms until the 1950s, when Hammond E. Chaffetz, a senior partner, began implementing the changes that altered the structure of the firm forever. He is almost solely responsible for moving Kirkland & Ellis from local to national prominence.

Chaffetz believed that investing in young legal talent would result in an increased client base. In a 1978 speech he said, "I learned very early that the way to attract and hold good clients is to surround oneself with top talent who can be counted on to

Left to right: James L. Palenchar, Bruce A. Featherstone, Frank Cicero, Jr., Donald E. Scott, and Andrew J. Petrie.

inspire confidence on the part of the clients. In reality, the great success of the firm is largely attributable to our intensive recruiting efforts and the outstanding new lawyers whom we have brought into the firm."

The firm's rigorous recruitment policy is in operation today. Lawyers in the Denver office alone include graduates from 23 law schools across the country.

Because new talent is rewarded aggressively, the partner-to-associate margin is much narrower at Kirkland & Ellis than at other firms. Currently there are 11 partners and 34 associates at the Denver office, 155 partners and 242 associates nationwide.

The term senior partner is a misnomer at Kirkland & Ellis. The partnership is young—leaders are in their late thirties to mid-forties.

Kirkland & Ellis has earned a reputation for bold litigation. The firm was featured in James B. Stewart's *The Partners* (Simon and Schuster 1983) as one of 12 firms "which occupy the pinnacle of the profession."

A significant portion of the firm's practice is in the corporate/securities, real estate, litigation, and financial services areas. Kirkland & Ellis lawyers practice in the federal and state courts and before federal and state agencies throughout the country.

The firm specializes in complex technological issues in addition to critical business and financial questions. Kirkland & Ellis prides itself on the efficiency and cost-effectiveness of its lawyers and support personnel. The firm works closely with its clients to control legal expenses.

Kirkland & Ellis is a single partnership governed by a committee of partners from all five offices. Major decisions affecting associates in the Denver, Chicago, Washington, Los Angeles, and New York offices are made by the partners in each respective office.

Lawyers in all offices of the firm frequently work together on various client matters. Principals at Kirkland & Ellis credit this working relationship as having enabled them to provide an unusual breadth of experience in serving regional clients whose interests and needs are nationwide in scope.

Long & Jaudon, P.C.

Lawrence A. Long began practicing law in Denver shortly after the end of World War II. In 1946 the young serviceman stationed at Buckley Air Force Base decided to make his home and his practice here. Long practiced both as a sole practitioner and with associates, many of whom are now among Denver's most prominent lawyers. He entered into a partnership with Joseph C. Jaudon in 1967, and since then Long & Jaudon has emphasized civil trials and the representation of individual and commercial interests in civil matters.

After being located in the Symes building for many years, Long was the first tenant in Denver's original "high rise," the Denver Club Building, and later the firm was the first tenant in what was then called the Energy Center.

In 1981 Long & Jaudon purchased the Bailey Mansion, becoming one of the first law firms to move out of the downtown area into Capitol Hill. Moving involved a certain amount of risk, but the partners agreed that if the move allowed the preservation of a historic building, rather than its destruction, relocating was worth the gamble. Restoration to the exterior and interior original finish of the 10,000-square-foot mansion, which had been on the National Register of Historic Places since 1978, was a labor of love which created one of Denver's most unique and elegant law offices.

Soon afterward other professional businesses began moving to the Capitol Hill area, and it is now considered a prime business and residential real estate area. In 1984 Long & Jaudon converted the mansion's Carriage House into offices. Two years later the firm purchased and restored the adjacent historic Flower Mansion.

With room to grow came a change in philosophy. "We decided to expand and broaden our base," says Fred Long, son of founder Lawrence Long. The firm continues its civil litigation practice and emphasizes insurance defense, wills, estates, corporate law, real estate, commercial litigation, workers' compensation, and personal injury practice.

Firm founders Lawrence A. Long (left) and Joseph C. Jaudon.

Because of the range of specialties practiced at the firm, communication between attorneys is critical. The professional staff meets once a week to discuss cases. A weekly round table was designed to spur questions and create dialogue. Thus, cases are evaluated with a broad range of input, and members of the firm have a forum to gain information and insight from each other.

Lawrence Long retired from the practice of law after nearly 50 years of active trial work. Called the "father of the Denver Botanic Gardens," he continues to serve as a member of the Board of Trustees. "It's my pride and joy," he says of the famous gardens whose roots were literally buried in the once-vacant field behind his Denver home.

Lawrence Long instilled a "spirit of giving back to the community," says his son, "and to this day, the firm is very conscious of the privilege of practicing law in Denver."

The firm's office, the Bailey Mansion, as it appeared following the completion of restoration efforts.

Sherman & Howard

In 1892 a young lawyer from Philadelphia stepped off the train in Denver. As James H. Pershing descended the steel steps, he took in his first glimpse of the "capital of the West." He saw a bustling frontier town poised to become a thriving city; the silver panic had not yet begun, the cornerstone of the Colorado State Capitol had just been laid, the newly opened Brown Palace Hotel was doing a prosperous business, and the fledgling Denver Bar Association, only a year before, had commenced on a century of service to its members.

Young Pershing was a farsighted man. He recognized the West's opportunities in natural resources and real estate and the importance of capital formation to the growth of the region. Most importantly, he saw the necessity of high-

Winston Howard. Photo courtesy of De Croce Studio

quality people if the West was to fulfill its promise.

Pershing commenced his practice in Denver in January 1892. Some of the West's finest lawyers joined with him over his 50 years of practice so that when he died, shortly after the end of World War II, one of Colorado's oldest law firms carried on. The name partners changed nine times over the past century, chronicling the growth of the firm that became Sherman & Howard, a multicapable legal resource serving clients not only throughout the West, but also the world.

Throughout its history, Sherman & Howard had within its walls many individual lawyers who were responsible for making much of Colorado's legal history; lawyers whose legal skills included advocacy and counseling from the law of water and mining claims to municipal and

Samuel Sherman. Photo courtesy of De Croce Studio

corporate finance and who were equally at home in mountain ranches and city skyscrapers.

The firm grew rapidly from the dozen or so lawyers that survived Pershing. It doubled in size in each of the decades after Pershing's death and expanded its practice into five other cities in the West. Sherman & Howard continued to serve legal needs in municipal and corporate finance, all aspects of business law, taxation, real estate and natural resources, and added new specialties including employment law, environmental issues, telecommunications, and aerospace. Sherman & Howard's priority, in its development as a regional law firm with worldwide capability, was to provide its clients with the finest in expert, knowledgeable service. The firm welcomed new demands resulting from economic changes and growth, while carrying on a tradition of specialized law practice.

While providing the finest in professional services, members of the firm also have been prominent in educational and civic affairs. Sherman & Howard has supported professional organizations (four of its partners served as president of the Denver Bar Association). The firm's *pro bono* work included first amendment censorship cases, economic development assistance for state and local projects, and public interest lawsuits. Several members of the firm teach in their specialty at the University of Colorado or University of Denver law schools.

Sherman & Howard epitomizes a problem-solving approach of the practice of law, grounded in the reality of a century of practical application and adapted to the changing needs of its clients.

Tilly & Graves, P.C.

Tilly & Graves, P.C., is a Colorado law firm that does most of its litigating across state lines.

The firm's practice specialty is counseling national and multi-national companies in preparation for complex litigation and organizing the defense effort. It acts as national and regional counsel, which involves many of the firm's litigation teams in trials in jurisdictions outside Colorado. Classically, one or associate lawyers. Additional staff includes paralegals with specialized training, professional administrators, secretaries, and clerical assistants.

As the scope of corporate and carrier liability has grown, the firm has expanded into complex litigation, often in multi-district settings, principally in matters involving pharmaceutical, environmental, industrial, and agricultural product dispatch, but without sacrificing the interests of our clients. This often requires skillful negotiation and procedures outside the courtroom setting," says Harmon Graves, senior shareholder.

Charles Socha, a diplomate of the National Board of Trial Advocacy, adds, "There is no better service to a client than thorough preparation based on an intelligent analysis of the issues involved. That, we find, is the ultimate deterrent to protracted litigation."

Tilly & Graves, P.C., utilizes state-of-the-art technology for in-house cataloging of scientific literature and documents in litigation. The firm is so technologically oriented that it is often called upon by associated firms and clients to provide guidance in the establishment of computerized data bases and document-retrieval systems.

"While technology has forever transformed the practice of law, the discovery process has altered the nature of litigation," says Graves. "Although the discovery process has taken much of the surprise element from a trial, it can make lawsuits prohibitively expensive. Selective discovery with the consent of our clients has in proper cases reduced some of the burden."

While its growth reflects a dominant role in its chosen fields, Tilly & Graves, P.C., strives to maintain a sense of small-firm collegiality among all levels of lawyers and staff.

Harmon S. Graves in the firm's reception area.

two lawyers and two or three paralegals comprise the field team for a case. The field team is supported by other lawyers and paralegals remaining in Denver.

From modest beginnings in 1952, Tilly & Graves, P.C., has grown to 86 employees. Of 28 lawyers, 13 are now shareholders and 15 are liability issues. The firm has maintained its strength and interest in aviation law, workers' compensation, casualty insurance, surety law, personal injury, and professional liability matters.

Tilly & Graves, P.C., recognizes the value in avoiding courtroom resolution. "While a substantial number of cases require resolution through the courts, we are ever mindful of the need to end disputes with

Zisman & Ingraham

Sanford Zisman and James Ingraham first met while on opposite sides of an IRS estate tax audit. They soon discovered a mutual respect for one another's technical expertise in the tax field, which eventually led to their joining forces January 1, 1986, to form Zisman & Ingraham, P.C. Not surprisingly, the firm specializes in tax, probate, estate planning, wills, and trusts.

"Sandy" Zisman, a tax lawyer, and a CPA by background, worked for a nationally recognized tax lawyer in California upon graduation from the N.Y.U. law school graduate tax program. After returning to Colorado in 1966, he practiced as a sole practitioner specializing in tax and estate planning.

After graduating from the University of Maryland School of Law in 1966, Jim Ingraham began his legal career with the Internal Revenue Service in Washington, D.C., where he worked as an estate tax attorney with the IRS Office of International Operations. He transferred to the Denver district in 1973 and in 1976 he became the manager of the Estate and Gift Tax Examination Group where he served for 10 years before entering private law practice.

Because of his IRS background, Ingraham is a frequent lecturer at Continuing Legal Education and Bar Association sponsored seminars on estate, gift, and generation-skipping tax topics, and IRS examination procedures. He is often called upon by other lawyers to act as a consultant in federal estate tax cases and occasionally serves as an expert witness.

Even though the firm does some income tax planning, particularly for closely held corporations, its emphasis is on estate planning and probate administration. Although a majority of the clients of the firm are people who live in urban areas, an important sub-specialty of the practice involves estate planning for ranchers and farmers.

A tax lawyer's expertise and the vast financial data which Colorado State University Extension Service accumulates are the elements for sound estate planning for farmers and ranchers. Since 1972 C.S.U.'s farm management economists and extension agents and Zisman have spent many hours discussing how best to handle the gamut of tax, financial, and personal concerns of farm and ranch families in Colorado. "Two entirely different things make our practice fun for me," says Zisman. "One is the challenge of working with complex tax laws that are continually changing, and the other is the personal relationships I enjoy with my clients who live all over the state of Colorado."

Law partners Sanford Zisman (left) and James Ingraham

Law, Knous and Keithley

The firm's members from left to right: Roger Keithley, Merle Knous, John Law, and Garrett Tuttle.

The general practice of the law firm of Law, Knous and Keithley includes specializing in the defense of professional liability matters with a concentration in representing attorneys and health care professionals. The specialty arose from the escalating complexity of business affairs and the trend toward suing professionals and businesses. "When I started practice as attorney for Denver Tramway in 1951, I never saw a complaint against the company that was more than one-and-a-half pages long," says Merle Knous, who also remembers when briefs were three to six pages long. Law remembers when doctors, lawyers, and accountants were not target defendants.

Principals in the firm have more than 100 years of collective experience in the practice of law. John Law began practicing in 1951. He was affiliated with several firms, including the trial firm of Dickerson, Morrissey, Zarlengo and Dwyer, a premier Denver trial group. In 1957 he formed the partnership of Law, Nagel and Clark, which expanded to more than 14 lawyers in later years. In 1984 Law entered into partnership with his former University of Colorado Law School classmate, Merle Knous.

Merle Knous comes from a long line of public officeholders, the most famous of whom is his father, William Lee Knous, who served as chief justice of the Colorado Supreme Court and later as governor of Colorado. Merle Knous served as deputy and chief deputy district attorney, first assistant United States attorney, and later served as a Denver district judge for 10 years in the Second Judicial District in Denver. As a prosecutor, he personally tried in excess of 120 jury trials and 30 trials to court.

Roger Keithley, an astronautical engineer, was working in the aerospace industry when he took up the law. He spent two years as a trial attorney with the Denver regional office of the Securities and Exchange Commission (1974-1976). In 1986 he became "of counsel" to the firm of Law & Knous, and he became a partner in 1987. He handles professional malpractice actions and complex commercial cases, many of which arise from alleged violations of various provisions of the securities laws.

Three partners served their country in the military. Law was on active duty with the Navy during World War II and 30 years later retired as a Captain in the Naval Reserve. Knous served in the United States Air Force also during World War II as a flying officer in B25s and P-38s, and Keithley was with the U.S. Army.

Garrett Tuttle, the firm's newest member, joined Law, Knous and Keithley in 1987, after two years' experience as a law clerk for a judge of the Court of Appeals.

The lion's share of the firm's work is complex litigation. The scope of practice includes not only insurance defense but also representation of public and private employers in employment rights disputes.

McGuane & Malone

Thomas P. Malone (left) and Frank L. McGuane, Jr.

McGuane & Malone was founded on October 15, 1981, by Frank L. McGuane, Jr., and Thomas P. Malone. The partners-to-be knew one another by reputation in the Bar Association and from their mutual involvement in the Colorado Interdisciplinary Committee on Child Custody. What they didn't know about one another until they became partners was that both were graduates of Notre Dame.

Prior to founding the firm, McGuane was a sole practitioner, with a practice limited to divorce, custody, and related matters. Malone, in practice since 1974, found himself concentrating more and more on child custody cases. Together they decided that it made sense to create a boutique firm that specialized exclusively in matrimonial law.

The challenges inherent to matrimonial law are many. "The area of matrimonial law has become much more complicated," says McGuane. "You have to have experience in more areas of law than any other specialty I know of. First and foremost a good matrimonial practitioner must be a top-notch trial lawyer. He must not only keep up-to-date on constantly changing Colorado law, but also on the many federal laws and court cases that now affect divorcing families. The matrimonial lawyer must also be knowledgeable about taxation, securities, pensions, real estate, business entities, business and professional practice valuations, accounting, and more. And, of course, the divorce lawyer has to have a little psychologist in him/her."

Each case must be handled differently, which presents its own challenge. "Sometimes you need to be an alley fighter," says McGuane. "Other times, a gentle, conciliatory approach is more appropriate. You have to know which strategy to use when."

A fourth challenge is that clients come into the office with preconceptions about the process. The lawyer's job is to educate while meeting the client's other needs. "We try to get the client thinking as realistically as possible, to know that there are seldom clear-cut winners or losers," says Malone.

"Although Colorado has an exceptionally honest, high-quality judiciary, we really believe it's almost always best to settle out of court, where the client still has control over the outcome," explains Malone. "Of course, there are instances when going to court is the only way to accomplish a client's objectives or to satisfy his or her needs."

The firm's goals are as challenging as the practice itself. McGuane & Malone aspires to be the best matrimonial law firm in Colorado—lawyers' lawyers, always better prepared and more knowledgeable on the facts and law than the opposition, on top of the current state of the law, and best able to settle the case on the most advantageous basis for the client, or to take it to trial if necessary.

Happy 100th Birthday, Denver Bar Association; we are proud to be part of you!!

Klaas & Law

Bruce Klaas found a wife and a mansion through the want ads. In 1975 Klaas glimpsed a newspaper ad stating that the Consulate Mansion, a magnificent historical building that housed the French consulate in the 1960s, was for sale. The property was being marketed by Mary C. Rae, a well-known Denver real estate agent. Klaas purchased the mansion in 1975 and married Rae on Valentine's Day, 1984. Today husband and wife carry on their respective professions from the mansion's offices.

Klaas' career began with a 1956 employment opportunity at General Motors Corporation in its patent, trademark, and copyright training office in Washington, D.C., while he earned his law degree at George Washington University. Upon graduation, he worked for GM from 1959-1961. He joined a private practice in Detroit in 1962 to further his career in patent, trademark, and copyright matters.

In 1971 Klaas moved to Denver, where he was instrumental in founding the firm of Edwards, Spangler, Wymore and Klaas. In 1974 he formed the firm of Klaas & Law with Richard D. Law. The firm specializes in patent, trademark, copyright, and unfair competition law. Current members of the firm include William P. O'Meara and Joseph J. Kelly.

One of the firm's first clients was the Adolph Coors Company, which pioneered the aluminum can and is a leader in can-manufacturing technology. Klaas & Law counseled Coors on patent matters involving can-manufacturing equipment. The firm also helped the company prevent its beer from being shipped unrefrigerated by unauthorized carriers. The case arose back in the days when bootlegging Coors beer cross-country by the truckload or trunkload was a common practice.

Scott's Liquid Gold was another of the firm's early clients. When Scott's Paper Products disputed the ownership of the name "Scott's," the firm had to track the history of the locally made product. In order to document that the furniture polish was used in Denver in the 1920s under the name Scott's, the firm ran an advertisement in the Denver newspapers asking for witnesses who knew about the furniture polish's roots. The firm hit the jackpot when one 75-year-old woman stepped forward to report that not only did she know the original furniture polish maker, named Scott, she had sold the product door-to-door starting in 1925.

Klaas is involved in the development and successful commercialization of several inventions, including the use of Minoxidil to promote hair growth. The product, which has been the subject of activities by the Upjohn Company, has resulted in substantial growth of Upjohn stock.

An avid athlete, Klaas helped found the Colorado Squash Racquet Association, and was primarily responsible for bringing Hashim Khan, the world's greatest squash player, to the Denver Athletic Club as its club pro.

Klaas is also actively involved in the American Intellectual Property Association and the United States Trademark Association, and serves on various bar association committees.

Holme Roberts & Owen

Holme Roberts & Owen is a law firm that cares—about its clients, about Colorado, and about quality. As one of Denver's oldest and largest law firms, it has grown up with the state and strives to make a difference in the quality of life for residents.

Established in 1898 to meet the demands of the growing Rocky Mountain frontier, HRO has from its beginning been involved in cases that are central to the growth of Colorado. At the turn of the century, the firm was primarily involved in mining, oil, and gas matters. As one of the West's most knowledgeable natural resources lawyers, Harold D. Roberts was a principal drafter of the Mineral Leasing Act of 1920, a foundation of modern oil and gas law.

Also an outstanding water lawyer, Roberts and the firm served as counsel in many areas that affected Denver's future. For example, the 23-mile tunnel that brings water from Dillon Reservoir on the western slope to Denver, nearly doubling the city's water supply, is called the "Harold D. Roberts Tunnel."

Today, with its headquarters occupying six floors in **One** United Bank Center in downtown Denver, the firm also has satellite offices in Boulder, Englewood, Colorado Springs, and Salt Lake City, and a European office recently opened in London. It has more than 200 attorneys.

As one of the fastest-growing firms in the region, HRO's practice is broad-based, and divided into four major areas: corporations, litigation, natural resources, and tax and estate planning.

There are approximately 60 lawyers within the corporations department whose practice involves general representation of corporations, partnerships, and other business entities, both large and small. This practice includes general business planning, mergers and acquisitions, tender offers, joint ventures, public and private equity and debt financings, municipal finance, real estate transactions, franchising and corporate reorganizations, bankruptcy, and liquidation proceedings. Clients include some of the largest companies headquartered in the state as well as start-up firms.

Some of the firm's work in the securities area is well-known to the general public. Examples are the recent $4-billion combination of United Cable Television Corporation with United Artists Communications, Inc., and the 1991 merger of United Banks of Colorado, Inc., into Norwest Corporation—the largest banking combination in Colorado history. Recently the firm also acted as counsel to The Anschutz Corporation and its subsidiary, Denver and Rio Grande Western Railroad Co., in the latter's acquisition of Southern Pacific Transportation Co., and to Adolph Coors Company in connection with several acquisitions and securities offerings.

Banking and commercial financing are significant parts of the firm's practice. Holme Roberts & Owen has enjoyed a relationship that spans nearly 90 years with United Banks of Colorado, Inc., the state's largest bank holding company, and its lead bank, United Bank of Denver, as well as the majority of its other 45 affiliates.

The firm's litigation department, managed by a five-partner council, is involved in the entire

A British Beefeater. Photo by Dave Jacobs courtesy of The Stock Broker

One United Bank Center. Photo by Robert Ashe

James E. Bye, chairman, Tax and Estate Planning Department.

Alaska, and has advised The Anschutz Corporation in negotiations for the unitization of the largest oil and gas deposit in the Overthrust Belt. Locally, the firm represents such national companies as Newmont Mining, Texasgulf, Shell Oil, Tenneco, and Exxon.

Lawyers in the firm's tax and estate planning department advise clients in acquisitions, divestitures, reorganizations, individual tax planning, and other areas. Its employee benefits and retirement plan group represents a number of private and public foundations and charitable trusts.

New and growing areas of emphasis for HRO include international law, venture practice, intellectual property, telecommunications, health care, and sports law. Paul Jacobs, a partner in the corporate department, is generally recognized as the driving force in forming the ownership group that was awarded a National League expansion franchise for major league play beginning in 1993.

Dedicated to professionalism and value for its clients, Holme Roberts & Owen offers its clients expertise and quality service. In recent years, in an effort to operate at maximum efficiency and cut client costs, the firm installed an advanced computer system and programs that set it apart from many other firms.

gamut of civil litigation. As HRO's largest department, it has developed groups of lawyers who emphasize practice in specific areas, such as antitrust, corporate, securities, contracts, employment discrimination (an area in which the firm has become very active), product liability, federal criminal defense, bankruptcy, and most other aspects of business law.

The environmental practice group of the litigation department handles toxic tort cases, civil penalty proceedings, and compliance matters. Significant cases include the representation of Shell Oil Company in connection with the Rocky Mountain Arsenal. The firm also represents Sinclair Oil, Martin Marietta, and Eagle-Picher Industries in environmental matters.

HRO began as a natural resources firm. Today its natural resources department handles oil and gas, mining, water, oil shale, solar energy, and uranium matters, and has gained a nationwide reputation for its expertise in large property acquisitions. For example, the firm has represented a corporation formed under the Alaska Native Claims Settlement Act in connection with exploration for hardrock minerals in

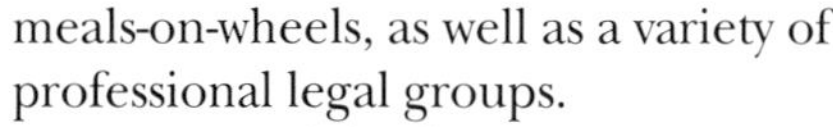

The Denver symphony. Photo by Keith Brofsky courtesy of The Stock Broker

"Race To Save The Planet" on public television and a supporter of the Boulder Symphony Orchestra, the Colorado Springs Fine Arts Center, and Ballet West in Salt Lake City, among others.

Holme Roberts & Owen also supports the community through a plethora of fund-raisers, law school scholarships, charitable contributions, and pro bono work. Its employees are encouraged to actively seek out organizations in which to volunteer their time and services. They include chambers of commerce, the American Red Cross, Volunteers of America, medical associations, and meals-on-wheels, as well as a variety of professional legal groups.

Many of the firm's members are also teachers, authors, and nationally known experts in their given fields. The chairman of the litigation department is the former dean of the University of Denver College of Law and two of Colorado's Federal Court judges are former litigation partners of the firm. Harold Bloomenthal is nationally known as an expert on securities law and has written numerous books on the subject. He recently developed a computer system capable of tracking the Blue Sky Laws of all 50 states and producing reports appropriate to a client's facts.

The firm is a democratic place to work. Its executive committee sets the major policies that govern its operation. Day-to-day activities are supervised by a management committee appointed by the executive committee. Associates are given the opportunity to serve as members of committees in order to become involved in the decision-making process at an early stage. The firm strives to create a working environment that is challenging, supportive, and friendly.

Holme Roberts & Owen is a firm whose history is steeped in heritage. It is a firm that is dedicated to the state's growth and vitality. As an important part of Colorado's past and present, HRO will continue to help make a difference in the quality of life of its clients and the communities it serves.

Through the use of modems and other state-of-the-art software, the firm has the ability to communicate, translate, and transmit virtually all documents electronically.

"We are a firm that changes as our client's needs change," explains Jim Owen, who is one of the senior partners. "We recognized that law today is as much a business as it is a profession. The cost-effective delivery of our services is one of the objectives of our firm."

HRO is a firm that has taken an aggressive and visible posture in the marketplace during the past few years. Its activities reach out to the communities that have mirrored its growth. It is involved in a variety of marketing and philanthropic activities. An ad developed in conjunction with the 1990 Final Four basketball tournament held in Denver featured the headline "At Crunch Time, Give Us the Ball." The firm is a local sponsor of "American Playhouse" and

Daniel S. Hoffman, chairman, Litigation Department.

MONTGOMERY
LITTLE
YOUNG
CAMPBELL
& McGREW
ATTORNEYS AT LAW

Montgomery Little Young Campbell & McGrew

Montgomery Little Young Campbell & McGrew celebrated its 25th anniversary in 1990. Robert R. Montgomery started his own practice in 1959 upon graduation from the University of Colorado College of Law. The young attorney's legal career got off to an inauspicious start; Montgomery said he began with "no money and no prospects." In 1965 he joined forces with David Little, who had been working in the prosecutor's office, and Montgomery Little was born. Shortly after the firm's founding, Roy E. Montgomery, Robert's father, brought his insurance and estate experience to the practice.

In 1968 Bayard Young's partner was appointed to the District bench, so Young brought his name and trial practice to Montgomery Little & Young. Dan McGrew, a CPA prior to graduating law school, signed on in 1974. As the Montgomery Little Young & McGrew practice developed, the firm needed banking and real estate expertise. It found those services in the person of Richard Campbell, who brought his real estate acumen to the firm in 1974.

Montgomery Little Young Campbell & McGrew has grown steadily over the years, flourishing even during tough economic times when other firms were forced to scale back their operations. It presently operates with 30 attorneys and 50 staff employees. Montgomery says, "Every five years we've moved. And every time we've moved, we've said, 'This is the last time.'"

The firm has expanded its practice into all areas of law to include antitrust, employment, environmental, real estate, banking, transactional, bankruptcy, franchising, natural resources, and family law. To a degree, Denver's economic climate has dictated the firm's areas of expansion. For example, the bankruptcy practice came on strong when the transactional practice began fading during Denver's oil bust years. Most of the firm's antitrust work is in the field of medicine, but its antitrust practice is not confined to the health care industry.

The firm has developed a strong condemnation practice. Richard Campbell litigated the first Denver International Airport condemnation case. The firm's client was initially offered $11 million for property on the proposed airport site, but Campbell argued successfully that $40 million was more fair.

Like most successful firms, Montgomery Little Young Campbell & McGrew has had its share of important cases, but Montgomery says, "the sweetest victories are simply winning for the client, regardless of the amount of money involved."

Although the firm started out primarily as a defense firm, it now handles both sides of a case. "When we made the decision to be an all-purpose law firm, the competition changed," says Montgomery. The firm began competing with larger firms. "We think we can offer clients better representation for less money.

"We answer phone calls, we're efficient, and we don't travel in threes," Montgomery says. "For a number of years, people believed that the higher the hourly rate, the better the law firm. They know better than that now. People want value for their money."

Montgomery Little Young Campbell & McGrew trial lawyers go to any lengths for their clients, says Montgomery. "We can take it all the way to trial as needed, and the other firms know it," he says, pointing out that bluffing rarely works in litigation.

Montgomery has noted many changes in the practice of law over the years. Notable among them is the increased complexity of society that makes it difficult for a person to get through life without having to consult an attorney. "When I started practicing law, people could go their entire life without seeing a lawyer," he says.

In addition to their contributions to the firm, Montgomery cites members' diverse civic contributions and causes, which run the gamut from politics to pollution. Montgomery is active in environmental concerns primarily related to the nuclear industry. Campbell serves on the board of trustees of Regis College, Jonathon Gordon is the founding director of the Hospice of St. John, and Perry Nissler is a Littleton city councilman, to name a few.

The firm's goals for the future include continued growth as necessary. Montgomery says, "Our goal has always been to deliver the best legal service at a fair price. If that fosters growth, then we're ready."

Radetsky & Shapiro

The law firm of Radetsky & Shapiro was founded in 1985, when Steven Shapiro joined Jay Radetsky in Radetsky's established Cherry Creek practice. The full-service firm specializes in commercial litigation, personal injury litigation, real estate, banking, corporate practice, domestic law, and wills and trusts, with a particular preference for high-end litigation and complex cases. Within the scope of the personal injury practice, the firm conducts more motorcycle accident litigation than any other firm in Colorado.

Radetsky's practice nearly spans the spectrum of legal representation. He moves from commercial litigation to domestic relations to real estate transactions to loan workouts with equal aplomb. He has practiced for 16 years and still welcomes new matters as each offers unique challenges and opportunities to help someone in need while utilizing his wide-ranging legal skills.

Shapiro's work is 85 percent personal injury, with the accent on personal. The clients are thought of first and the staff of attorneys get in-volved with their client's lives, and to a great extent, with their futures. Because of the interpersonal nature of personal injury litigation, Radetsky & Shapiro believes it's hard to look at the profession as a business. The founders believe that if it ever gets to a point where it's just a business, they don't want to do it anymore.

While the firm takes great pride in the ongoing representation of large organizations and handling their specialized needs, it also believes in standing up for the "little guy." For more than a year Radetsky has been involved in a case surrounding an 85-year-old woman who was bilked out of her life savings by an unethical homebuilder. Although the firm helped the woman gain a judgment against the builder, the case is far from over because the builder has vanished. Even though the firm has yet to collect a fee, it will continue to fight for her rights. In another case, the firm represented a small auto repair shop that was fighting "city hall" by challenging an ordinance that threatened its livelihood.

Seated left to right: Daphne Wells, Deborah Dore, and Kathy Kobel. Standing left to right in the second row: Jay Radetsky, Lorraine Mollohan, Jillann Dubue, Mary Hall, Patricia Bakke, Jennifer Donaldson, and Steven Shapiro. Standing left to right in the back row: Jeffrey Ludwig, Patrick Augustine, Donna McLellan, Cindy Beston, Kathleen Terran, James Edwards, and Celia Foegen.

The firm also champions personal rights issues. Radetsky & Shapiro played an integral part in changing the laws regarding sovereign immunity with regard to compliance standards that must be met when suing governmental entities.

The firm's motto has been, "If you do good work, more work will come." The rapid growth of the firm attests to its adherence to that motto. Radetsky & Shapiro currently operates with 7 attorneys and 10 support staff personnel. The firm would like to stay at about that size as they want to maintain a family atmosphere.

What Radetsky & Shapiro would like people to know about the firm is that it strives for the highest standards and that it sacrifices those standards for no one.

Attorneys' Title Guaranty Fund, Inc.

The purchase of a home is probably the biggest transaction an individual will make in his or her lifetime. Buyers and sellers greatly benefit from the assistance and guidance of legal counsel due to the diverse issues involved in such a transaction.

Recognizing this, Attorneys' Title operates according to four very simple maxims: First, to protect client interests, real estate titles must be examined by experienced real estate attorneys; second, an attorney must be provided a means to insure a client against risk at nominal cost; third, an attorney must be able to provide this insurance as a routine professional service to a client; and fourth, attorneys must assure that professional services remain available and affordable to the public.

Realizing the importance of the attorney's role in real estate transactions, Bar-related® title insurance was founded in Florida in 1947. The Florida Fund was created out of the need to provide the real estate attorney with a source from which to obtain accurate and current title information.

This concept was nurtured by prominent attorneys throughout Colorado in the late 1950s. George M. Gibson was at the forefront of the early development of Bar-related® title insurance in Colorado. He and a small contingent of Colorado attorneys fostered the corporation operating today in Colorado, Utah, North Dakota, and Minnesota.

The Fund, as it is referred to by member attorney agents, was incorporated on October 11, 1960, and commenced doing business as Attorneys' Title Guaranty Fund, Inc., in January 1962. The organization was established so practicing attorneys could provide their clients with title insurance based upon an attorney's professional title evaluation.

Fundamental to the introduction of this concept was the idea that

To better serve their clients, attorneys work closely with them to ensure that they receive expert counsel. Photo courtesy of David Lissy

real estate practitioners have a professional obligation to counsel clients about all ramifications of a given real estate transaction. Both buyer and seller need the advice of independent counsel to explain the limits of coverage to assure that the client is receiving the most protection available. In order to identify the issues that may have long-term consequences, an attorney should be involved in every step of the real estate transaction.

Title commitments and policies of Bar-related® companies are generally issued by member attorney-agents directly from their law offices. Searches are performed either by the lawyers, the lawyers' staffs, or by Attorneys' Title Guaranty Fund, Inc. In 1968 the Colorado office of Attorneys' Title made a substantial financial investment to become a shareholder in the SKLD Title plant, an independent title plant.

The scope of computerized title information expands daily to provide quicker and more efficient title information. Today, a simple phone call to Attorneys' Title can provide extensive data on most real estate in Colorado. The company also utilizes several other computer systems to generate closing documents, track accounting information, and assist the title plant in disseminating information and endorsements.

Bar-related® companies maintain a high standard of underwriting excellence as demonstrated by their low claims rates. One factor behind the low rate is that the issuing lawyer, because of his or her close involvement with the interested parties, has a more extensive knowledge of the facts than records alone can indicate. Thus many possible title problems are eliminated.

Because real estate transactions affect many legal rights, including estate planning, tax matters, and income and investment management matters, Attorneys' Title advocates consultation with a lawyer when purchasing or selling real estate. One goal of Attorneys' Title is to assure the availability of independent legal services to the public in real estate transactions at a reasonable cost.

The staff at Attorneys' Title Guaranty Fund, Inc., is dedicated to providing clients with professional and efficient service. Photo courtesy of David Lissy

This is accomplished by giving real estate lawyers the ability to provide title insurance services as part of their legal services in real estate transactions.

Attorneys' Title also conducts closings on behalf of members at any location. Members can contact the closing department, and arrange the preparation of closing figures, HUD-1s, settlement statements, escrows, wire transfers, or for simply handling disbursements. In 1989 Attorneys' Title achieved great public awareness as a contractor for HUD, handling closings in the Denver metropolitan area.

Attorneys' Title also introduced the Colorado Fund Link and Fund Net programs in 1989. Fund Link is a program designed to match the legal expertise of the real estate attorney with the legal needs of the real estate broker. Through the program, Realtors® can obtain a list of member attorneys available to assist them in contract drafting, contract negotiations, contract review, closing, and ultimately the issuance of title insurance. Fund Net, short for Fund Network, is a statewide network of real estate attorneys and specialists that provides a resource of real estate information for consumers and member attorneys.

Attorneys' Title also maintains ongoing educational programs including the Real Property Round Table series. These programs are created to educate members about essential areas of real property and to discuss important issues and trends in the industry. Attorneys' Title feels the Fund is well positioned for the future, with flexible member services to meet the needs of a changing marketplace and the means to carry its tradition of service, support, and quality into the next century.

Horowitz & Berrett

Jay Horowitz defines the practice of law as "the process of developing most thoroughly, creatively, and persuasively those facts that make your client's position invulnerable." The former federal prosecutor made the government's case invulnerable when, as assistant special prosecutor under Archibald Cox and Leon Jaworski during the Watergate trials, his work led to the indictment of several key Nixon aides.

Established in 1980, Horowitz & Berrett is a litigation-only practice that specializes in sophisticated, complex commercial litigation. David Berrett has practiced law in Colorado since 1978, specializing in commercial litigation. Horowitz moved to Denver in 1976. In addition to his Watergate background, he also served as Assistant United States Attorney for the Southern District of New York (Manhattan).

To a great extent the focus of the firm's practice is an outgrowth of Horowitz's years as a federal prosecutor, where the types of cases he handled concerned commercial transactions. The most well-known of these cases arose from President Nixon's reporting of charitable contribution income tax deductions arising from his gifting his vice-presidential papers to the government.

This earlier work is similar to the work Horowitz & Berrett does now; it is heavily factual in orientation. While the firm's personality tends to be more prosecutorial because of the backgrounds of its principals, it represents plaintiffs and defendants. Dave Berrett confirms that the firm's background and litigation philosophy make the firm more aggressive regardless of the client's designated position in a case. Horowitz & Berrett engages in securities, real estate, corporate, and partnership litigation, and its practice includes the prosecution and defense of professional malpractice claims and the representation of persons who are subjects of criminal investigation/prosecution.

Horowitz & Berrett principally litigates in Colorado, but also has handled litigations in Nebraska, Iowa, Kansas, Nevada, California, and elsewhere.

Attorneys are often accused of using theatrics, but it is the Horowitz & Berrett support staff who has the theatrical bent. After office hours are over, the staff performs with the Hunger Artists Ensemble Theatre, an underground theater group touted as the best local company in Denver.

Horowitz augments his practice with the classroom, teaching trial tactics and advocacy to lawyers and also teaching law students at the University of Denver College of Law, while Berrett is extremely active in community affairs.

Left to right: David M. Berrett and Jay S. Horowitz

Abramovitz, Merriam & Shaw

Abramovitz, Merriam & Shaw was established to defend taxpayers in disputes with government. Tax specialists Michael J. Abramovitz and Ted H. Merriam founded the firm in 1987, and Ralph W. Shaw joined them in 1989. While most firms try to handle tax controversies under the umbrella of general tax law, Abramovitz, Merriam & Shaw makes tax controversy the core of its practice, with an emphasis on civil and criminal tax trials and federal and state audits, appeals, and tax collections.

"We think there is intrinsic value in protecting clients from government," Abramovitz says. "People need to know that there is someone on their side." The firm is an ardent adversary of the Internal Revenue Service as an institution, but has an intelligent respect for the government's attorneys. A good working relationship with the government's agents and lawyers is an essential element of the firm. "We decide what we're going to fight about and get on with it. We don't waste their time or ours," says Abramovitz.

Left to right: Michael Abramovitz, Ted H. Merriam, and Ralph W. Shaw.

Left to right: Michael Abramovitz, Ralph W. Shaw (standing), and Ted H. Merriam.

Tax controversy defense requires confrontational deftness, knowledge of tax accounting, and an eye for detail. "Most trial people are generalists—not detail-oriented. Most tax people take a noncontroversial, highly technical approach," says Ralph Shaw. "Hybrids like us are far less common. We combine the best of both worlds."

Ted H. Merriam, also an adjunct professor at the graduate tax program of the University of Denver law school, grew up during the Vietnam era and has "a healthy unease of government." Boredom with a general law practice motivated him to return to law school where he earned a master's degree in tax. The marriage between trial experience and tax education makes him one of the hybrids Shaw described.

Ralph Shaw owned and operated his own pension consulting business prior to attending law school. While at the University of Denver College of Law, he handled pro bono tax controversy cases for indigents. His ERISA (Employee Retirement Income Security Act) expertise broadened the firm's scope of practice when he signed on in 1989.

Abramovitz went to law school after working as a mathematician. He found both tax and criminal law interesting—the more complex the better. In 1973 he joined the firm, which became Drexler, Wald & Abramovitz. While there he became aware of the need for a specialized tax controversy firm in the Denver area, and his experience became the firm's nucleus.

Says Abramovitz, "It is absolutely vital for citizens to know that there is someone who will aggressively defend them against the IRS. The government may be fair most of the time, but if an exception occurs, there is someone here to protect the citizen."

Kutak Rock & Campbell

The contemporary art that lines the halls and offices of Kutak Rock & Campbell expresses with bold strokes, strong colors, and unique materials the personality of the firm—young, bold, creative, and innovative.

Kutak Rock & Campbell was established in 1965 by Robert J. Kutak, Harold R. Rock, and William G. Campbell in Omaha, Nebraska. In the 25 years since, the one-city, three-lawyer practice has grown into a multicity operation of more than 200 attorneys. By 1980 Kutak Rock & Campbell was the third-fastest growing law firm in the nation, with offices in Denver, Omaha, Washington, D.C., and Atlanta. The Denver office was founded on January 1, 1977.

Kutak said in an address to a legal seminar that although the firm is equally committed to growth and excellence, "we are seeking to build not a law practice, but a law firm. Whatever success we have had arose out of the idea that it is more important to have quality lawyers than a long list of clients."

Kutak Rock & Campbell's principal areas of practice are finance, litigation, and commercial transactions. The finance practice fueled the firm's initial growth, and the firm has represented more than half of the *Fortune* 500 corporations nationwide. The Denver office has represented every significant investment banking organization in the metropolitan area.

Kutak Rock & Campbell pioneered the development of financing techniques that have become industry standards. For example, the firm developed a technique to finance low- and moderate-income housing that provides funds for approximately one-third of all first-time home buyers throughout the country. And it structured the first limited partnership financing to be

Senior partners (left to right) John H. Bernstein, Robert D. Irvin, James D. Arundel, and Paul E. Belitz.

Managing partner James D. Arundel.

registered and publicly traded. A leader in municipal finance, the firm performs a substantial amount of tax counseling on large municipal projects, representing parties in intricate corporate or project financing.

Kutak Rock & Campbell serves as counsel in many complex corporate and commercial litigation matters, including environmental, employment discrimination, corporate reorganization, creditor representation, financial institution representation, and bankruptcies. Bond workouts are a specialty of the firm. A substantial part of the firm's litigation practice involves the defense of actions brought against national brokerage firms in alleged securities fraud cases.

Like any large firm, Kutak Rock & Campbell has had its share of precedent-setting cases involving a wide spectrum of issues. The firm served as counsel for the first corporate guaranty insurance company in a transaction that involved the largest investment of capital in a new insurance company. The firm also served as counsel for the first case to consider the constitutionality of mandatory AIDS testing for public employees.

Kutak Rock & Campbell has a unique charter that emphasizes the importance of mutual respect, trust, fairness, and selflessness among all lawyers, associated professionals, and staff members. All lawyers in the firm are encouraged to become experts in areas of interest to them as they conduct its practice. A commitment to providing opportunities to enrich the intellectual life of its lawyers and staff is central to the firm's philosophy. *Fortune* magazine wrote that Kutak Rock & Campbell "may be the most democratically managed large legal firm anywhere."

The partnership at Kutak Rock & Campbell is young. The firm believes that with youth comes entrepreneurial effort and innovation. "Kutak Rock & Campbell emphasizes a practical, yet creative, approach to problem solving, but innovation is by no means its sole

province. Every engagement begins with a clear recognition of established customs and consideration of whether they can be adapted to meet the client's present need."

The firm's practice demands that its lawyers stay abreast of developments in government and business. Kutak Rock & Campbell meets this challenge by employing non-lawyer specialists in a range of disciplines. Accountants, government affairs specialists, and others broaden the firm's service.

Each Kutak Rock & Campbell office operates autonomously, a unique aspect of its operation among national firms. Autonomous does not mean independent, however, and each office has the capacity to network with every other office via WangNet. In this way attorneys can marshal support from other offices electronically and instantaneously.

Kutak often admonished members of his firm to "dream no small dreams." Part of Kutak's dream was for the firm to become a strong presence in the national and international communities. It has. His personal dream was to make lawyering an art form. He did.

For nearly six years, Robert Kutak was the driving force behind the ABA Commission on Evaluation of Professional Standards—often referred to as the Kutak Commission—which drafted the Model Rules of Professional Conduct, which Kutak liked to call "the law of lawyering."

At the time of his death, the *New York Times* called Kutak "a fresh breeze in legal circles, a cyclone actually." In his memory the firm established The Robert J. Kutak Foundation. The Foundation focuses its philanthropy on areas of particular interest to him, including the enhancement of education; training, and research in the legal profession; professional ethics; and the encouragement of young artists.

Knutson, Brightwell, Reeves & Oldham, P.C.

Modern mining is a global enterprise and Denver is its axis—the geographic hub of the United States for minerals. National and international natural resource companies have their offices here even if their mines are elsewhere.

Knutson, Brightwell, Reeves & Oldham serves a transcontinental clientele from its Denver office. As general counsel to numerous public and private natural resource companies, the firm specializes in mineral finance matters, public land law, and ever-increasing permitting and environmental work.

The firm's strength is the considerable and diverse expertise of its directors. Rodney D. Knutson, an electrical engineer, represents companies exploring for, developing, and financing hardrock mineral deposits. He also counsels oil and gas exploration development companies.

Left to right: George E. Reeves, Thomas P. Brightwell, Kenneth R. Oldham, and Rodney D. Knutson. Photo by Sara Frances.

Knutson has been involved with the Rocky Mountain Mineral Law Foundation as a member, trustee, and executive committee member. He has written numerous articles analyzing industry problems, and has served on the planning committee for numerous mineral and tax conferences.

Mining is an extremely capital-intensive field where complex multinational transactions are commonplace, and tax or business expertise is essential. Thomas P. Brightwell provides that expertise. An accountant and an authority in the fields of domestic and international business law, he was a professor and director of the Graduate Tax and Natural Resource programs at the University of Denver from 1967 to 1980. During this time he also served as a consultant to several law firms in the fields of taxation, business planning, securities law, and natural resources law. After leaving the university he served as Manager of Tax Planning for a multinational natural resources company. He remains actively involved in Continu-

ing Legal Education programs.

Since 1966 George E. Reeves has been engaged in private practice in Phoenix, San Francisco, and Denver. His experience encompasses a broad scope of real property and title law. His mining law practice extends from the location, maintenance, and patenting of mining claims to the milling, smelting, and sale of ores, minerals, concentrates, and metals. An expert on all phases of mining, he has written numerous articles and books and is frequently called upon in a consultant capacity.

Prior to joining the firm in 1988, Kenneth R. Oldham served for almost two decades as general counsel and vice president of the Rocky Mountain Energy Company. His background is eclectic—he served as counselor to management, as a negotiator and draftsman of complex business arrangements, and as an active participant in large-scale litigation. He was also in charge of planning and implementing regulatory and legislative strategies at the federal and state levels.

Oldham is credited with organizing and administering a pioneering Environmental Services Department that secured hundreds of mining, milling, and reclamation permits and licenses.

The firm is active in numerous professional organizations, including the Colorado Mining Association, the Northwest Mining Association, the Colorado Hazardous Waste Management Society, the American Institute of Mining Engineers, and the Rocky Mountain Mineral Law Foundation.

Johnson, Ruddy, Norman & McConaty

While some people have skeletons in their closets, Johnson, Ruddy, Norman & McConaty has one in its conference room. The firm's practice concentrates on the defense of physicians in medical malpractice cases, and the grinning skeleton helps the attorneys explain difficult medical concepts to juries. They expend great effort developing the medical background and complex medical issues on a case so they are able to crystallize the pertinent information and make it easily understandable to a jury.

The skeleton helps. But the most critical component of the practice is the expertise and experience of the lawyers, a number of whom are doctors as well as attorneys. Dr. Roger F. Johnson, a physician-attorney, founded the firm in 1970 in response to a need in the medical community for medicolegal expertise. As the practice grew, other attorneys with medical malpractice

Left to right: Roger F. Johnson, M.D., Brian G. McConaty, Robert Ruddy, and Collie E. Norman.

experience were added to the firm, including other physician-attorneys, as well as those skilled in related fields. Today the practice encompasses litigation regarding insurance and medical-legal matters, as well as personal injury.

A surge in medical malpractice cases began in the early 1980s, and the firm has been involved in the defense of more than 1,000 malpractice defense cases since that time. The Colorado legislature's tort reform acts of 1986 and 1988 greatly impacted cases within the practice, as have legislative maneuvers addressing litigation requirements and settlement limits.

Johnson, Ruddy, Norman & McConaty attorneys practice in a highly complex field where experience is everything. Roger Johnson, a doctor with 25 years of medical malpractice experience, is on active staff at Denver General Hospital and is the former director of Emergency Medical Services there. Johnson is a staff physician at Swedish Medical

Center and serves as medical-legal consultant to Colorado Medical Society, DG, and Presbyterian Medical Center.

Robert Ruddy, a former deputy district attorney for the First Judicial District of Colorado, joined the firm in 1981. He has been involved with numerous complex medical malpractice, product liability, and personal injury claims for both defendant and plaintiff.

Collie Norman, a former special agent for the Office of the Inspector General at the Pentagon, concentrated on investigating aircraft crash and medical malpractice litigation. Norman joined the firm in 1984. He has extensive trial and medical malpractice experience.

Brian McConaty, a former deputy district attorney in both Aspen and Denver, served as Assistant United States Attorney in charge of the narcotics prosecution unit before joining the firm in 1983. He has lectured on numerous medical malpractice topics before various legal and medical organizations and is in the process of publishing a book on preparing physicians for deposition. McConaty is also an assistant clinical professor in the Department of Medicine at the University of Colorado Health Sciences Center, where Roger Johnson, is also on the clinical teaching faculty.

The firm is frequently called upon to give expert testimony and opinions on medical malpractice issues to governmental bodies as well as to speak to various professional, civic, and community groups.

Lowery, Lamb & Lowery, P.C.

Philip E. Lowery is one of Denver's best-known and most controversial trial lawyers. His trademark is the more than 100 pairs of fancy western boots he wears with jeans (in his office) or with expensive silk suits (in the courtroom). His is a familiar face on the 10 o'clock news, and his clients run the gamut from the famous, such as billionaire businessman Adnan Khashoggi, to the infamous, such as securities dealer Meyer Blinder.

"I love trial work; the controversy doesn't bother me at all," he says. "Also, I think that it's one of the few professions where you can really help people."

To get to the offices of Lowery, Lamb & Lowery, you step into the elevator at the Petroleum Club Building and press the button marked "Lowery." The penthouse office decor strays from standard-issue legal library adornments. Bold modern art shares wall space with African wildlife photographs from one of Lowery's safaris. An old RCA Victor television (one of the first color televisions ever made) rests on the native Colorado sandstone fireplace wall.

Lowery says he's loosened the legal profession up a bit. "We're people," he says, "We represent people. We ought to act like it."

Born and raised in poverty in Braman, Oklahoma, Lowery says he always wanted to be a trial lawyer because one of the richest men in town was a lawyer. "They lived in the biggest house," he recalls. "Mine had a dirt floor in it. When I finished high school, I got on a bus and never went back."

In the early 1960s Lowery shared office space with Richard Lamm. The two ran for the state legislature together and got elected in 1966. Lowery served one term. Lamm went on to become governor.

Lowery founded Lowery, Lamb & Lowery in 1961. He built his firm the way he built his reputation, expending equal parts of ego, expertise, and elbow grease. The firm, which specializes in trial litigation, has expanded across the western United States and now includes more than 60 employees and represents some of the largest *Fortune* 500 companies in the world.

Lowery says he won clients by winning cases. Jimmy Ju, owner of the New China Restaurant, was Lowery's first client. Leo Payne was his second. Lowery, representing Ju, sued Payne, who was impressed enough to hire Lowery later as his own attorney.

His most exciting civil case was fighting a Chicago bank's efforts to foreclose on a ranch, for which Lowery won his client $32 million in 1984.

Lowery says his goals were achieved a long time ago. He still appears in court at least once a week, works 12 to 14 hours a day, and says he enjoys it more than ever. "My motivations in the last two or three years have changed. A lot of the stuff we do, we do pro bono. I think it's important to help people who need help."

Philip E. Lowery.

A pair of alligator skin boots in midnight blue, one of several pairs in Philip E. Lowery's extensive collection.

Rothgerber, Appel, Powers & Johnson

Founded in Denver in 1903, Rothgerber, Appel, Powers & Johnson is one of the largest law firms in the Rocky Mountain region, with nearly 70 attorneys. The firm has a diversified commercial and litigation practice, with expertise in most major areas of the law.

The partnership of Rothgerber and Appel was formed by Ira C. Rothgerber and Walter M. Appel, boyhood friends and roommates at the University of Colorado School of Law. In 1903 they rented offices in the Ernst and Cranmer Building at 17th and Curtis streets. Three years later, in 1906, the partners moved to the Symes Building at 16th and Champa, the firm's location for the next 52 years.

In 1935 Ira C. Rothgerber, Jr., joined the firm following graduation from the University of Colorado School of Law, and while serving overseas during World War II met a New Jersey lawyer, William S. Powers, who joined the firm as a partner in 1946. Continuing the family tradition, Walter's son, Robert S. Appel, was invited to join the firm in 1952 upon graduation from the University of Denver College of Law.

The firm has enjoyed steady, managed growth during the second half of the twentieth century.

"A booming economy, such as Denver experienced in the 1970s, is not sufficient reason for expansion," explains Ira C. Rothgerber, Jr. "Nor is growth just for the sake of growth. Above all else, it is our desire to provide our clients with superior legal service which determines the shape of our practice."

That philosophy, which places a premium on personal service, continues to serve the firm well. Each client is assigned a lead attorney who serves as the primary contact within the firm, and other attorneys are assigned depending on the scope of the engagement. Rothgerber, Appel, Powers & Johnson has the resources of a sizable firm, yet is able to provide each client with individual attention.

The firm's practice includes both transactional and litigation expertise. More than half of the attorneys are actively involved in litigation, practicing before state and federal courts and regulatory agencies. Transactional clients include all types of organizations in all stages of evolution.

The firm provides both ongoing counsel and single matter representation to local, regional, national, and international organizations.

Today's complex legal environment requires innovative strategies coupled with proven technical competence, and the firm expects the practice of law to change just as rapidly in the next 50 years as it has in the last. Rothgerber, Appel, Powers & Johnson believes that by combining its proven expertise with creative problem solving, it can meet the challenges of the next century.

An early illustration of the Daniels & Fisher Tower, presently near the offices of Rothgerber, Appel, Powers & Johnson, on the 16th Street Mall. Photo courtesy of the Colorado Historical Society

Zapiler & Ferris

With offices in Cherry Creek and Colorado Springs, partners Steven M. Zapiler and John P. Ferris practice exclusively in the area of personal injury law. To those who know these dynamic men, their success is no surprise. "The basic ideals of integrity, liberty, and democracy are protected by the American jury

the participants are willing to remember that a speedy and fair compromise serves not only the client, but serves the community as well, then the system can have a positive effect for everyone involved." For Ferris, the practice of law is a way to bring out the best in people when the worst has happened, a way to make a differ-

ple, and Ferris founded a local golf tournament to support the Colorado Youth at Risk program, a program endorsed by President George Bush and designed to turn the tide of juvenile delinquency.

Zapiler & Ferris has combined leading-edge computer technology with old-fashioned hard work and compassionate, caring attention to its clients. Ferris notes that one of the firm's greatest strengths is its team approach to the operations of the office, fully incorporating every member of the staff in the management process. "Our ability to serve our clients and our community with excellence is built upon the foundation of a coordinated team effort of people who believe they can make a difference."

John P. Ferris (left) and Steven M. Zapiler (right) were both chief coordinators of the community trial advocacy law clinic at the University of Denver.

system, and respect for the process, the court, and other trial lawyers is an opportunity to make a real contribution to the system," according to Zapiler. "I learned as a young man that trial lawyers are, and have always been, keepers of the flame of equity for all. To make sure that justice will be afforded equally to every injured citizen is a sacred responsibility."

Ferris brings with him a master's degree in education and a broad background of life experience. He believes the advocacy system must be one that leaves all parties satisfied if it is to live up to its promise. "If all of

ence. "It is a trial lawyer's role to help the injured victims receive fair compensation, and to empower them to get on with their lives and learn how to overcome even the most difficult circumstances. When my eye is on the future of our clients' lives, I know that I have contributed something to the community."

Zapiler and Ferris, both graduates of the University of Denver College of Law, were also chief coordinators of the community trial advocacy law clinic, first founded at DU in 1904. Both are active in the Colorado Trial Lawyers Association, and they share a dedication to the future of the community through youth. Zapiler is a frequent lecturer in schools and facilities for young peo-

The philosophy at Zapiler & Ferris is that a law firm should act as a coordinated team dedicated to excellent legal representation.

Paralegal Associates of Denver, Inc.

The term "paralegal" first appeared in the late 1960s to define a separate position in the legal profession. Prior to that time, overworked attorneys would rely heavily on their experienced secretaries to take on some of their legal work, thereby creating overworked secretaries. Legal professionals gradually realized there was a niche between the attorney and the secretary where a trained paraprofessional could perform the tasks routinely performed by the attorney, relieving the attorney of some work load and allowing the secretary to tend to his or her normal duties.

Today the profession is mature, experienced, and invaluable. "The paralegal profession is essential to the cost-effective delivery of legal services; an indispensable, efficient tool," says Joanna Hughbanks, founder of Paralegal Associates of Denver, Inc.

Hughbanks became interested in the paralegal profession in 1973 after a car accident placed her in the middle of a lawsuit. She worked as a paralegal for sole practioners for four years, and then began pursuing temporary contracts with several attorneys. She worked alone for some time until increased demand for temporary paralegal services prompted her to hire other paralegals to work as independent contractors. Hughbanks & Associates was born.

In 1985, Hughbanks incorporated the business as Paralegal Associates of Denver, Inc., and the concept of contract paralegal services grew. She has built a national reputation as an expert in complex civil litigation management, and the firm, with more than 50 paralegals, has a national clientele. The firm's specialty is managing civil suits from filing to completion.

Hughbanks says the firm's success rests firmly on the experienced shoulders of its paralegals. Paralegal Associates works primarily with paralegals who have a minimum of three

Joanna Hughbanks, founder of Paralegal Associates of Denver, Inc.

years' experience. Their abilities to perform certain tasks are thoroughly tested before they are given an assignment. "We don't just provide bodies— we match the person's past experience with the expertise required for the current job," says Hughbanks.

Temporary paralegal services are often used by firms during peak work periods or for special projects. For example, in litigation they may be utilized for long- or short-term case management; document review, analysis, and coding; deposition summaries; trial preparation and assistance in trial. Another example of a peak work period need is during the preparation of closing a client's corporate merger or acquisition. Anytime a firm's full-fime staff is unable to devote the time necessary to accomplish the tasks required, a contract paralegal may be the answer.

Contract temporaries allow firms to expand their staff without increasing overhead and without having to screen and hire new employees. The cost of employment are absorbed by the paralegal service, not the firm. The firm is also relieved of the responsibility of keeping that employee busy and billing when the need is no longer there.

Computerization has changed the way law firms operate, and Paralegal Associates paralegals are familiar with a variety of software used in litigation document management. In addition, the firm uses database programs that provide a cost-effective method of document control and retrieval for firms that do not have their own computers. The programs can be redesigned to meet individual client or case requirements.

Although most of the demand for temporary paralegals is in the area of litigation, Paralegal Associates provides paralegals in real estate, bankruptcy, environmental matters, natural resources, contract review, corporate, and securities.

Hughbanks has tracked the paralegal profession's evolution over the past 20 years, and believes one facet remains constant—its challenge. "Paralegals are responsible for digging up facts and determining where information may be found. One of the most attractive aspects of the profession is that we're always learning something new."

Leventhal & Bogue, P.C.

Jim Leventhal and Jeff Bogue formed the law firm of Leventhal and Bogue, P.C., in 1983. They will tell you they are trial lawyers and not litigators; a distinction important to them because both of them have extensive trial experience. Leventhal started his legal life in 1975 as a public defender. Bogue is a former U.S. Attorney. The law firm, which now consists of five lawyers, is a perfect example of lawyers in the passionate pursuit of justice.

Leventhal was attracted to the challenges of personal injury law. Leventhal and Bogue lawyers have taken on large corporations, physicians, and state and local governments, as well as giant insurance companies. "The people in this firm are driven to help individuals who have suffered serious, disabling injuries," Leventhal says. "We think of ourselves as equalizers to ensure that powerful corporations and individuals do not trample our clients."

The five lawyers in the firm—

Left to right: Bruce J. Kaye, Natalie Brown, Jeffrey A. Bogue, Victoria J. Koury, and Jim Leventhal.

Jim Leventhal, Jeff Bogue, Bruce Kaye, Victoria Koury, and Natalie Brown—are experienced and aggressive trial lawyers. The law firm represented individuals who were catastrophically injured when the lift at Keystone collapsed. Its lawyers have been involved in complex products liability cases against large corporations such as Volvo resulting in multimillion-dollar verdicts on behalf of seriously injured clients.

The lawyers from Leventhal and Bogue, P.C., are among the most active trial lawyers in the state of Colorado. "We probably try as many, if not more, lawsuits than any other firm in Denver," Leventhal says. The firm also specializes in professional malpractice, workers' compensation, and criminal law.

Bruce Kaye is a 1974 law school graduate. He started his career with the District Attorney's office in Boulder before relocating to Grand Junction where he established his own law firm. He joined Leventhal and Bogue, P.C., in 1987. Kaye was lead attorney in the lawsuit against the division of Volvo resulting in a multi-million-dollar verdict for a client

who suffered a traumatic amputation as a result of a defective product. He limits his practice to products liability, personal injury, and workers' compensation.

Victoria Koury came to the firm after leading the Jefferson County office of the Colorado Public Defenders Office for five years. She was named Colorado Public Defender of the Year in 1987 and has a strong civil and criminal background. Natalie Brown joined the firm in 1986. Her practice includes personal injury, medical malpractice, and recreational torts such as hiking and skiing accidents.

The firm's philosophy is twofold; it seeks to guarantee that justice is served and to prevent the same tragedy from striking another innocent victim. For example, in a landmark ski case against Aspen Highlands, the resort was forced to redesign a portion of a run where numerous skiers were seriously injured. The impetus for change was Leventhal and Bogue's lawsuit against the resort on behalf of its client, who was paralyzed when she lost control and hit a tree in the exact area where numerous other skiers had been injured.

Leventhal and Bogue, P.C., is a strong advocate of the jury system and is actively involved in the battle to keep intact a citizen's rights to have a fair trial by jury. "We believe jurors won't compromise justice. Everyone has a right to take a dispute before other citizens and have that jury evaluate it and make a decision. Anybody who tampers with that system is tampering with democracy."

Ireland, Stapleton, Pryor & Pascoe

Established in 1926, Ireland, Stapleton, Pryor & Pascoe is one of Denver's pioneer law firms. From the beginning, the firm has set itself apart by forging close working relationships with clients, understanding their businesses, and personally attending to their needs. In doing so, the firm has helped shape the face of Colorado and, over the years, has gained a reputation as a business builder.

The firm has helped nurture numerous small companies into successful institutions. Lloyd King, founder of the $1.6-billion-a-year King Soopers grocery chain, became a client in 1937. At the start, King owned just one market—and lived above it. Ireland, Stapleton, Pryor & Pascoe represented King Soopers from its humble beginnings to its current 65-store operation.

Senior partner Ben Stapleton says one of the firm's serious commitments (and great joys) is helping small business ventures develop into major operations. That tradition has continued through the years, with the firm representing emerging companies in one of the most active venture-capital/high technology corporate practices in the Rocky Mountain region.

Ireland, Stapleton, Pryor & Pascoe has a diverse practice in corporate law, representing public and privately held companies engaged in manufacturing, retailing, telecommunications, software development, and numerous other industries in the Rocky Mountain region. The firm maintains a varied commercial finance practice, being especially active in the front-end structuring of complex transactions, such as credits including Eurodollar facilities, banker's acceptances, letters of credit, and venture capital fund investments, and in credits with specialized collateral, such as livestock, ski facilities, and intellectual property.

Real estate, land use, and environmental law are important practice areas for the firm. Ireland, Stapleton, Pryor & Pascoe has helped its clients achieve a major municipal annexation, participated in the writing of new and innovative zoning codes, created legal structures for low-income housing development, and helped in the planning and financing of substantial projects such as shopping centers, office buildings, and resort developments. Recently it successfully negotiated a workout for a client of more than $100 million in property debt taken over by the Resolution Trust Corporation.

Ireland, Stapleton, Pryor & Pascoe is oriented toward complex litigation as well. The firm has an extensive and varied practice covering virtually all areas of substantive law, such as antitrust, bankruptcy, white-collar crime, construction, environmental, financial, insurance, labor, natural resources, products liability, securities, and taxation. While the firm's lawyers handle cases of all sizes, complex litigation has become a substantial part of its practice, involving such recent matters as aviation disasters, asbestos contamination, lender liability, securities fraud, and land use.

The needs of businesses for the sophisticated services of experienced corporate attorneys like those at Ireland, Stapleton, Pryor & Pascoe continue to grow.

Ireland, Stapleton, Pryor & Pascoe's approach to the practice of law in today's competitive and complex world is simple. "We're problem solvers, first and foremost," is the often-repeated theme as the shareholders of Ireland, Stapleton, Pryor & Pascoe meet annually for a long weekend of business planning and assessing new directions of the law.

Last year Ireland, Stapleton, Pryor & Pascoe served more than 600 clients. The firm is lean and aggressive, with 35 attorneys practicing law in the full range of substantive areas usually associated with much larger commercial firms. The firm believes that with fewer lawyers, it can provide more responsive and efficient attention to its clients' needs.

Ireland, Stapleton, Pryor & Pascoe rests its success ultimately on its people—lawyers, paralegals, and support staff—including leaders in the legal profession and in the Denver community. These experts get results for clients through thoughtful legal analysis and, in many instances, by drawing on their local knowledge and community ties.

Ben Stapleton is the son of the Denver mayor after whom Stapleton International Airport is named. He served for 23 years as the chairman of the Colorado Water Conservation Board. Pryor was the assistant attorney general of Colorado from 1952 to 1956. Monte Pascoe was the president of the Board of Denver Water Commissioners from 1986 to 1989, and served as executive director of the Colorado Department of Natural Resources from 1980 to 1983.

ABOVE: Left to right: Monte Pascoe, Wilbur M. Pryor, and Benjamin F. Stapleton.

BELOW: Left to right: G. James Williams, Jr., William E. Tanis, Susan L. Oakes, Jack G. Lewis, and Lawrence P. Terrell.

Pendleton & Sabian

Vision, principally driven by the needs of its clients, describes the outlook and commitment of Pendleton & Sabian, P.C., attorneys and counselors at law. Vision is demonstrated in its willingness to take risks, look beyond the present, and anticipate the needs of a changing business climate. Vision is seen through client relationships characterized by problem solving, advocacy, and partnership. Vision is evident in its carefully managed growth, from two lawyers in 1970 to today's mid-size firm that tackles emerging areas of law. Finally, vision is an attitude, the way Pendleton & Sabian views problems as opportunities, increasing its capacity to develop solutions.

Joining backgrounds in real estate, business, and securities law, Brian Pendleton and Michael Sabian founded the firm in 1970. It now has a thriving commercial law practice providing comprehensive services to a broad base of business, institutional, and individual clients. The firm serves Colorado clients, national and foreign companies operating in the

Members of Pendleton & Sabian's litigation and bankruptcy group. From left: Gary M. Clexton, John F. Simpson, Erin K. Toll, Joseph E. Meyer, Sue Ann Fitch, Stephen F. Collins, Patricia A. Motz, Michael E. Romero, and Alan C. Friedberg.

Rocky Mountain region and elsewhere in the country, and U.S. companies doing business abroad.

Pendleton & Sabian's practice is focused on all areas of commercial law, including business and tax planning and organization, real estate, natural resources and environmental law, securities and other financing, financial institutions, governmental regulations and administrative law, and bankruptcy and workouts.

Its highly experienced civil trial lawyers handle complex litigation cases ranging from securities fraud to construction disputes to products liability. Personal injury and professional malpractice cases are also selectively undertaken. Pendleton & Sabian's work in the international trade arena stems from its early identification of Denver as a potential international business hub.

During the early 1980s the firm began to strategically position itself in an area traditionally dominated by much larger firms. In place of size it offered international clientele a refreshing mix of personal and professional service, providing accessibility, responsiveness, and the ability to accomplish given tasks efficiently.

Initially representing foreign investors in connection with real es-

tate and oil and gas ventures in the United States, the firm has attracted clients associated with high technology, financial services, and other types of natural resources.

With Denver's growth as an international headquarters, Pendleton & Sabian now has clients from or that conduct business in more than 15 countries, including Australia, New Zealand, Japan, Mexico, and several countries in Europe.

This international presence is enhanced by related activities. One firm member, Robert Wilson, is director and officer of the Australian/American Chamber of Commerce (Rocky Mountain Region). Brian Pendleton, fluent in French, studies Japanese and related cultural etiquette. A new associate is fluent in Russian and has a high degree of interest in Eastern European trade matters.

As an experiment, the firm hired an Australian chartered accountant to help service Australian clients and develop new business. Although he has since left, the firm believes these kinds of activities make it a better service provider. Its Pacific Rim team, involved in imports and exports, launched *Inbound*, a client newsletter that highlights legal developments involving imports due to a lack of local information concerning such matters.

Environmental law is another growth area of the firm, ranging from EPA Superfund litigation to permitting to land use. The firm emphasizes assistance and preventive counsel in areas such as compliance, groundwater contamination, and environmental-impact statement preparation.

Prominent developers, major lenders, and title insurance compa-

Brian Pendleton (left) and Michael A. Sabian, founders of Pendleton & Sabian, P.C.

As part of the firm's transactions group, (from left) Keith Crouch, Felice F. Furst, Jeffrey R. Fiske, and John F. Simpson serve a regional, national, and international clientele's natural resources and environmental law needs.

nies are among the firm's real estate clients. As Brian Pendleton's specialty, real estate has historically been a major practice area. Matters range from acquisitions and land planning to the development of residential and commercial subdivisions, shopping centers, hotels, and office buildings. Besides urban areas, the firm represents clients in nearly all of Colorado's mountain resort areas. With clients in the cable television, paging, and telephone industries, Pendleton & Sabian is developing a broad range of capabilities in the expanding field of telecommunications.

The negotiation of agreements relating to the development of oil, gas, gold, silver, and other minerals is representative of its natural resources practice. The firm continues to have an extensive practice in this area in spite of declines in oil and gas activity. Still other growth areas are intellectual property law, evolving antitrust law, new product development, advanced technology, health care, and copyright, trademark, and trade se-

cret protection.

Ongoing quality and mutually beneficial client relationships are constantly being nurtured. According to Brian Pendleton, the firm views itself as a problem solver. "Our goal is to establish effective client relationships through activities that build a value-added dimension to our services," he says. The firm stresses cost-effective, high-quality work, providing skilled negotiations and other services in both business transactions and litigation. It is committed to pursuing clients' objectives within the bounds of legitimate business concerns and applicable professional and ethical guidelines.

These goals and others are set forth in Pendleton & Sabian's mission statement, designed to instill its approach to excellence in client service and to strategically position itself

The firm's transactions group provides a broad range of services to the business and real estate communities. From left: Felice F. Furst, Richard F. Hennessey (managing director), Robert F. Wilson, Michael A. Sabian, Scott H. Culley, Gerald K. McGaugh, Brian Pendleton, and Ranelle T. Gregory.

in today's business environment.

Its size is advantageous when cases demand the immediate attention of lawyers proficient in specific disciplines. Free of cumbersome hierarchy, the firm quickly mobilizes attorneys to serve on project teams. Virtually all work is performed through a team approach.

The typical Pendleton & Sabian attorney has credentials and experience that go beyond basic lawyering skills. The staff includes two former deputy attorney generals, a former staff assistant to President Ford, and many who have authored legal articles and general business advice articles.

Recognizing the need to stay at the forefront of legal and business issues, the firm's lawyers participate in its ambitious education program featuring both in-house training and professional courses not limited to legal topics. An example is a firmwide networking technology seminar designed to help attorneys maximize assistance to clients in nonlegal matters as well as identify business opportunities.

Its mission statement also addresses community service. "We're a firm that has always believed in giving something back to the community," says Pendleton. Attorneys routinely take on pro bono cases and serve nonprofit organizations throughout the city.

Bigger is not necessarily better. Pendleton & Sabian is proof that a mid-size firm can succeed in areas traditionally reserved for large firms by being competitive and focusing on professional service. Its dynamic, adaptive, and forward-thinking style will ensure its distinctive position in the years to come.

Berenbaum & Weinshienk, P.C.

A panorama of Denver's skyline is the view from the modern offices of Berenbaum & Weinshienk, P.C.—a reminder of many projects the law firm has helped make possible in the city.

The original firm has been in business for **over** 50 years, and evolved into Berenbaum & Weinshienk, P.C., in 1983 by the merger of three firms. Berenbaum & Weinshienk, P.C., has achieved prominence in the metropolitan Denver community and the state of Colorado. It is also a firm that pays unusual attention to its clients through its philosophy, which blends professionalism and interest in the fortunes of its clients through personal relationships.

Joseph Berenbaum, the firm's senior partner, celebrated his 50th year as an attorney in 1990. A man of high standards, he views the practice of law as a profession as well as a business. High on his list of achievements is his work over the years that has helped many businesses grow and prosper.

The steady growth of Berenbaum & Weinshienk required a recent move to larger offices in downtown Denver. Its staff of lawyers, paralegals, and other support staff comprise a growing group which is presently more than 60 people. It is a full-service firm with the capacity to provide a broad range of sophisticated legal services. The firm's practice extends throughout Colorado and the United States and includes various foreign countries.

While general business and real estate—both development and lending—were originally the firm's niche, its client base and practice now encompass bankruptcies, commercial litigation, commercial lending, foreclosures, loan workouts, mergers and acquisitions, venture capital investments, private securities offerings, tax and corporate planning, environmental matters, labor laws, and trusts and estates.

Clients of Berenbaum & Weinshienk range from individuals and start-up companies to leading Denver business establishments, large national corporations, and international firms doing business in the Rocky Mountain region. They include well-known banks and mortgage companies such as Lomas Mortgage USA and Mellon Bank; local and national real estate developers and brokerage firms such as O'Connell Development

Berenbaum & Weinshienk has represented developers and lenders for many commercial and residential real estate projects in Colorado such as Founders Village, a large planned community in Castle Rock, Colorado, developed by Park Homes. Meeting with Park Homes representatives Gene Myers (second from right) and Cheri Litzinger (second from left) are firm members James L. Kurtz-Phelan, H. Michael Miller and Joseph Berenbaum.

Company, Park Homes, and Olympia York Cherry Creek Company; and a wide range of securities and venture capital firms and industrial firms and businesses that include The Columbine Venture Funds, Gates & Sons, Inc., Stanley Works, and Confederation Life Insurance Company.

The firm has seen many of its clients evolve from humble beginnings into major regional and national companies. Berenbaum & Weinshienk takes pride in its role in their growth.

Responding to an increasingly litigious society, the firm has a growing and well-rounded litigation department. Besides traditional commercial litigation arising out of real estate and other commercial transactions, the firm's experienced attorneys represent both plaintiffs and defendants in national and in-

Berenbaum & Weinshienk provides a full range of personal and business tax advice and planning, as well as general corporate representation. Attorneys Dan Sciullo, Elizabeth Myers and Steve Hoth meet with two of the firm's clients, Gordon Gates, president of Gates & Sons, Inc., and his wife to discuss their personal and business financial planning needs.

Joseph Borus, head of Berenbaum & Weinshienk's corporate department, and Amy Therese Loper, a shareholder of the firm, meet with Mark Kimmel, one of the firm's venture capital clients, to review a private placement memorandum outside Columbine's offices overlooking the Front Range of the Rocky Mountains.

tions, and international commerce are rapidly emerging law areas for Berenbaum & Weinshienk. Clients include foreign companies doing business in Colorado as well as American companies overseas.

The firm has carefully managed its growth to avoid the anonymity that can become a part of large organizations. It emphasizes a highly personal and comfortable internal atmosphere that extends to its client relationships.

Fiscally responsible and committed to staying debt-free, Berenbaum & Weinshienk prides itself on client fees that are truly representative of its services. "We combine high-quality work on complex issues with personal relationships with clients," says Michael Miller, managing partner. "Internally, we foster an atmosphere of cooperation and teamwork instead of competition, so our attorneys aren't always vying to get to the top of the ladder." Undue competitiveness among lawyers can often breed client overbilling, he says.

The firm's philosophy of developing the " whole lawyer" is carried out by stressing the more subtle and subjective aspects of the lawyer/client relationship. In contrast to being outside technicians or advisers, Berenbaum & Weinshienk attorneys become integral parts of their clients' teams to ensure their business objectives are being met.

A high percentage of the firm's attorneys are shareholders. Young attorneys are hired with the expectation they will someday be named **shareholders. A mentor** system allows each associate to work closely with a **shareholder. All attorneys** are expected to develop new business as well as to maintain strong personal and business relationships with existing ones. "We're not on an assembly line—we're here to help our clients achieve their business goals. It is important they are comfortable with our attorneys from both a personal and professional standpoint," says Miller.

Berenbaum & Weinshienk enters the 1990s in full contrast to an increasingly impersonal society. Its emphasis on confidence and trust in client relationships, combined with the expertise to handle complex business transactions, is a refreshing approach to the practice of law.

ternational business disputes, lender liability claims, labor matters, construction and mechanics' lien disputes, securities, and personal injury matters. Bankruptcy proceedings involving complex reorganizations and tort defense on behalf of self-insured businesses also constitute an important part of the firm's litigation work.

Berenbaum & Weinshienk has been involved in some of the largest bankruptcies in Colorado. In bankruptcy proceedings, the firm views its role from both a legal and business standpoint, with the goal of maximizing repayment when representing creditors and keeping companies alive and in operation through the restructuring of debts and assets when representing debtors.

Environmental regulation and hazardous waste cleanup, new financial markets such as telecommunica-

Berenbaum & Weinshienk always strives to resolve disputes expeditiously and economically for its clients. Four of the firm's litigation and bankruptcy attorneys, I.H. Kaiser, Martin Buckley, Ed Perlmutter, and Fran Cetrulo, discuss arbitration and mediation alternatives for dispute resolution with William Neighbors and Richard Dana, two of the principal arbitrators with the Judicial Arbiter Group at JAG's new offices located at JP Plaza in the lower downtown Denver historic district.

Carpenter & Klatskin, P.C.

Carpenter & Klatskin was founded by Willis Carpenter and Andrew Klatskin in 1978. Most of the firm's practice is in real estate law.

Willis Carpenter practiced with a mid-size firm in the Denver Club Building from 1954 to 1967 but didn't start concentrating on real estate work until 1968, when he became a sole practitioner. During that time, until 1978, he shared office space with Roy Romer, who was then a land developer. "Roy didn't want to practice law anymore; he wanted to run his businesses, so I fell heir to some of his real estate practice," Carpenter says.

Andrew Klatskin grew up in New York and moved to Colorado in 1973. He worked for an apartment house developer for a year before working with Carpenter. He remembers that it was a good time to be involved in the Denver real estate industry; the foundation of the boom was just being poured.

During the 1970s and 1980s the firm represented raw land developers, city developers, and entrepreneurs. When the real estate market weakened, the firm had plenty of business trying to help clients work out their financial problems. "Our litigation practice increased as it always does in hard times," Klatskin says. The firm tries to limit its litigation practice to real estate or business-oriented matters.

The firm has a local practice that is mostly contained within the state's borders, but has represented international investors from around the globe. The partners think that the representation of foreign investors is going to have a significant impact in the area of real estate practice, similar to the effect environmental issues have had.

Ask Carpenter about the firm's famous cases and he'll tell you about clients with no money and serious problems. "I've discovered that the cases you remember, the cases you feel really good about, are not necessarily the big cases or the ones with large monetary rewards. They're the cases where we helped someone who was desperate. They are the most rewarding."

The firm's philosophy can be summed up in one word— "enjoy." "Since we've chosen to be lawyers as our life's work, we want the daily routine to be enjoyable for us and our clients, if possible. I can recall any number of times that I preferred Monday to Friday. Friday is the end of the week and I haven't gotten done all of the things I needed to get done. But Monday there's new hope. The point is, I love coming to work every day," Carpenter says.

Carpenter isn't the only one who loves coming to work. "We've been graced with capable and loyal employees who have devoted their entire working lives to this firm," Klatskin says, noting that they have not had to hire a legal secretary or paralegal for more than 14 years.

Carpenter is a past president of the Denver Bar Association and both he and Klatskin served as chair of the Colorado Bar Association's Real Estate Section. The firm devotes much of its time to bar association and CLE activities.

Standing left to right: Holly Hoxeng, Andy Klatskin, and Darlene Sturgis. Seated left to right: Will Carpenter, Priscilla Kimitch, and Max Minnig.

White & Steele, P.C.

Admitted to the bar in 1923, Lowell White was a pioneer Denver insurance lawyer and founding father of the longtime Denver firm, White & Steele, P.C. Walter Steele, admitted to practice in 1949, became White's partner on January 1, 1953, when the firm was formed.

White was the first Colorado member of the American College of Trial Lawyers in 1953. The firm gained a reputation as primarily an insurance defense firm. Over the years, the scope of its practice has broadened. Today White & Steele is a civil trial defense firm involved in litigation, with primary emphasis on defending personal injury, property damage, insurance, malpractice, and commercial and environmental lawsuits. "We represent parties in court in civil damage cases of all kinds," says Steele.

Denver history runs in Walter

Lowell White

Steele's blood. His great-grandfather was a physician during the Civil War. Steele Street in Denver is named for him. Walter Steele's grandfather was chief justice of the Colorado Supreme Court, and his father was a Denver district judge who served longer than any other judge in Colorado. Walter Steele carried on the family tradition by becoming the youngest president of the Colorado Bar Association in 1964.

The once-small firm operates its current practice with 30 lawyers. Steele credits some of the growth to the necessity for specialization, even within the umbrella of a civil trial law firm. "We have ski lawyers, workers' compensation lawyers, asbestos lawyers, and lawyers for just about any litigation specialty you could name." This is the result of what he calls the "litigation explosion."

Steele says, "I used to ski as a child. If you broke a bone on the ski slope, you never dreamed of suing anyone. That has all changed now, of course." White & Steele represents a number of ski areas and is involved in defending litigation for the ski industry. The firm represented Keystone Ski Resort in the 1985 ski lift disaster.

The firm has had its share of famous cases and clients in 38

Walter Steele

years, too many to chronicle, says Steele. But some stand out in his mind. He represented Elliot Roosevelt, Franklin Roosevelt's son, in litigation involving a ranch the president's son owned in Colorado. Also memorable to Steele are the significant cases involving new products. White & Steele represented the B.F. Goodrich Co. in the first "blowout" case that involved the quality and safety of a new product on the market—the tubeless tire. Goodrich prevailed in the case.

The firm's future goals include continued modest growth with expansion of the practice into additional areas of law, with particular emphasis on environmental and toxic product cases and commercial law. Development is the key to the firm's future, says Steele. "We must continue the development of our expertise, and keep up with new developments in the law." The firm will continue to utilize avenues of alternate dispute resolution (ADR) where it best serves the client.

Joseph H. Thibodeau, P.C.

Joseph H. Thibodeau, P.C., is a firm of four lawyers whose practice is limited to the administrative and judicial resolution of tax controversies, civil and criminal, state and federal.

Its founder, Joseph H. Thibodeau (A.B., History, Holy Cross, 1963; J.D., cum laude, University of Detroit, 1966), began practicing in 1966 as a trial attorney, under the attorney general's Honors Program, in the Tax Division of the United States Department of Justice. (He was one of nine selected in 1966 out of 1,800 applicants).

Joseph H. Thibodeau

Thereafter, in 1970, at the age of 28, he became the youngest legal advisor (to former Governor William G. Milliken) in the history of the state of Michigan.

He came to Denver and to private practice in 1972. After a two-year stint with a small Denver firm, he became a member of the executive committee of a firm of 100 lawyers with offices in several states.

In 1979, having seen practice from these varied perspectives, he decided to "try it on [his] own," eventually forming Joseph H. Thibodeau, P.C., and adding other lawyers, but "never aspiring to building the world's largest law firm ('I had already been a member of that firm in Washington')—just, hopefully, among the best at what we do."

Thibodeau is a member of the Michigan (1966), Colorado (1972), and Wyoming (1991) bars. He has received admission to practice before the bars of the United States Supreme Court, the 6th, 7th, 8th, 9th, and 10th circuits, the United States Tax Court, United States Claims Court, and more than two dozen (pro hac vice) United States district courts throughout the country.

He is active in the American Bar Association (tax, litigation, and criminal justice sections), for which he frequently writes and speaks. He is a member of the National Association of Criminal Defense Lawyers, is listed in *Best Lawyers in America* (1985-1991), and was recently honored with installation (1988) in the American College of Tax Counsel. Since 1983 Thibodeau has been an adjunct professor (civil and criminal tax procedure) in the University of Denver's Graduate Tax Program.

Asked how things have changed in his 25 years of practice, Thibodeau responded: "Our kind of practice, perhaps only representative of our times, has undergone cataclysmic change. Nowhere is this more evident than in the area of criminal defense, particularly so-called 'white collar' criminal defense. If the United States Supreme Court had its way in plenary fashion—which it seems hell-bent on getting—it would abolish the criminal defense bar tomorrow. Witness its most recent decision (in re: Paul McNeil) with respect to the interro-

gation of an accused in custody. As Mr. Justice Stevens said in dissent, the majority's decision hails 'an inquisitorial system that regards the defense lawyer as an impediment rather than a servant to the cause of justice.'

"It is truly, at one and the same time, a most exciting, yet terrifying, time to be alive as a lawyer in this country. Never before in our history has the defense lawyer been more desperately needed to stand tall between the onslaught of an overreaching government, obsessed with prosecution, conviction, and incarceration ('law and order') at any cost, and the citizen; between freedom and tyranny.

"At the same time, never before has the profession been under greater attack by that government, for example, with subpoenas on lawyers and pre-judgment government forfeiture of attorneys' fees—causing many excellent practitioners to flee to safer ground. Perhaps not surprisingly, these actions have been orchestrated by an attorney general of the United States who has opined (and so directed his charges within the Department of Justice to conduct themselves accordingly) that government lawyers are not bound by the rules of professional responsibility.

"At the same time, aggressive awakenings in the tax area—civil and criminal—are identifiable at the state level. Colorado has the most severe penalties of all of the states.

"So, I guess, in response to your question: 'How have things changed?', I'd say they've become exponentially more difficult and challenging. At the same time, the lawyer's role of service to society has become commensurately more crucially needed, and the opportunity for gratifying contribution more clearly ever-present."

First Interstate Bank

On October 22, 1891, David H. Moffat, Jr., president of The First National Bank of Denver, formed the International Trust Company. It was the first institution of its type established west of the Missouri River.

In addition to David Moffat, the original board of directors included Walter S. Cheesman, H.W. Hobson, E.L. Raymond, Moses Hallett, Chester S. Morey, Anthony Sweeney, M.E. Smith, William S. Jackson, Mahlon D. Thatcher, Sr., and Charles H. Dow. (Dow was the inventor of the famous "Dow Theory," co-founder of Dow, Jones and Co., and publisher of the first edition of the *Wall Street Journal* in 1889.)

In 1958 the International Trust Company and The First National Bank of Denver merged. In 1983 the bank was acquired by First Interstate Bancorp and became First Interstate Bank of Denver.

Throughout its history the Trust Division has been a leading provider of trust services in the Rocky Mountain region, and has enjoyed a close association with the legal community. Its reputation was built with an unwavering commitment to service and outstanding investment performance.

No. Amt.

Owner's Name Eugene Brown
PRINT your name in INK

Residence Street

(Occupation with what firm, or school and grade)

SAVINGS STAMP FOLDER
for holding Stamp Receipts issued through
AUTOMATIC RECEIVING TELLERS
Operated By
The International Trust Company
MEMBER FEDERAL RESERVE SYSTEM
Seventeenth and California Streets
DENVER, COLO.

A wise and rich man said: "If you can't Save money, you can't Succeed!"

WE WELCOME YOU AT OUR OFFICES

INTEREST AND SAFETY FOR YOUR SAVINGS

IF FOUND, RETURN TO OWNER OR TO US
NOT TRANSFERABLE

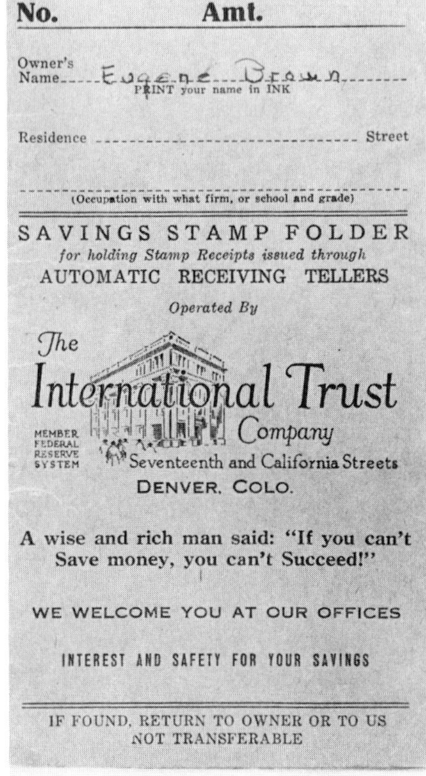

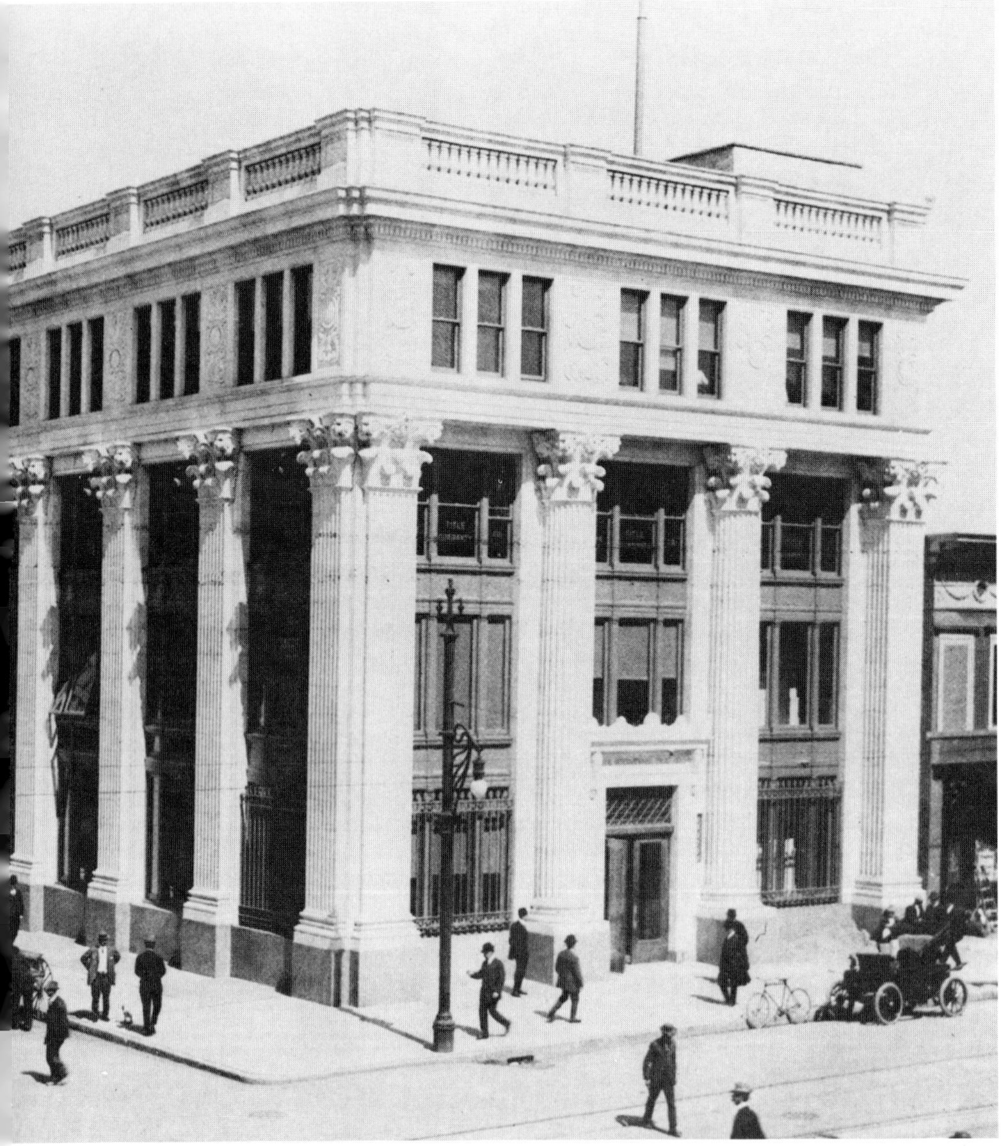

Mary Anstine, executive vice president and head of the Trust Division, believes the quality of an institution is a reflection of its people. "Our trust administrators have a long tenure with the bank. Their longevity and expertise enable us to provide a level of service that's unrivaled in this region. We are extremely attentive to the financial needs, concerns, and attitudes of each client. We listen. And then we tailor a portfolio to the individual customer's needs."

Today, the Trust Division manages over $5 billion in discretionary assets for individuals, corporations, and institutions, providing each client with the full benefit of a century of experience in the highly specialized field of trust services.

Blue Cross and Blue Shield of Colorado

Incorporated in 1938, Blue Cross of Colorado was founded to provide subscribers with a health care plan that utilized specified hospitals and doctors—the original preferred provider plan. The company sold its first plan to the May Company in 1938. The premium was 75 cents each month and covered nearly all fees. In its first year the company had 10 full-time employees and $50 in its petty cash fund.

In 1939 Blue Cross of Colorado processed 1,596 claims, all of which involved some length of hospital stay. For this, the company paid the hospital a grand total of $62,407, or approximately $39 per stay.

Blue Shield of Colorado, which

The headquarter offices of Blue Cross and Blue Shield of Colorado are located in Denver.

provides for doctor and medical care, was formed in 1942. The two companies merged in 1978 and became Blue Cross and Blue Shield of Colorado. The company, and the industry, grew at a phenomenal rate. Today 34,000 Coloradans earn a living in the health care field. The largest health coverage company in the state, Blue Cross and Blue Shield of Colorado is a vital part of the Col-

orado economy. More than $1.1 billion in claims is processed through the headquarter offices in Denver each year.

Blue Cross and Blue Shield of Colorado is not an insurance company, but a health coverage company that operates on a nonprofit basis, without stockholders. Eighty-five percent of its memberships are group plans.

Blue Cross and Blue Shield has offices across the United States. Prior to 1955 it was the only agency in the United States offering health care coverage. When other companies began to offer coverage, Blue Cross had to become more competitive, and that competition caused sweeping changes in the industry.

In the beginning all applicants were accepted for coverage regardless of health status. Every subscriber in a given area paid the same price for coverage, a practice known as "community rating." Enrollees with the poorest health risks were kept at the most affordable level possible because lower-risk enrollees subsidized the costs of higher-risk enrollees. As competition increased in the health insurance market, underwriting and rating practices similar to those traditionally used in other lines of business began to appear. Blue Cross and Blue Shield of Colorado continually works with each of their groups to ensure the lowest price possible for their members.

Another change that came about with increased competition was the emphasis on keeping people out of the hospital. Blue Cross and Blue Shield of Colorado was originally designed to take care of subscribers

when they were in the hospital, but it became apparent in the late 1960s that alternatives to hospitalization were more cost-effective.

Because of the company's strength, Blue Cross and Blue Shield of Colorado became the fiduciary agent for the Medicare program in Colorado in 1966, and has held that position ever since. In 1967 the company also won the bid to become the fiduciary agent for Medicaid, a combination state and federal health care program.

Blue Cross and Blue Shield of Colorado employees contribute significantly to the community. The Blue ACE (Active Community Enrichment) Team, composed of volunteers from the mailroom to the boardroom, works on special community projects. The company sponsors various health-related events that have included the March of Dimes Walk-a-thon, the Rocky Mountain Senior Games, quarterly blood donations drives, the installation of a health and nutrition series of films, and teachers' guides covering kindergarten through 12th grade in the public school systems in Colorado. Blue Cross and Blue Shield of Colorado also sponsored the fundraiser for the Denver Symphony for three years.

In addition, the health care coverage company sponsored two fitness and health-related super films at the Imax Theatre located in the Denver Museum of Natural History. More than one million persons of all ages viewed the film in 18 months.

Blue Cross and Blue Shield of Colorado is proud of its membership in the Colorado community that it has served since 1938. Through the years the company has been an innovator in health care programs for its subscribers and will continue to offer the best health care coverage available.